Praise For This Book

"Every couple should read this book!

"Money can't buy happiness, and for many couples money disagreements can pull them apart. Money is as much a part of a relationship as love.

"Marriage is a partnership that can end up on the rocks because of financial disagreements. If everyone in the country read *Couples and Money*, the divorce rate would plummet. It should be required reading for all couples applying for marriage licenses."

—Ginita Wall, CPA, CFP, Author and co-author of six leading books on financial and divorce concepts, including *The Way To Invest* (Henry Holt & Co.) and *Our Money, Our Selves* (Consumer Reports Books). Expert witness in the financial aspects of divorce and on the *Worth* magazine of top financial planners in the USA.

***

"*Couples and Money* is one of the few books in the field that give a practical and insightful roadmap that can help couples move from irrationality to sound money management. A wonderful, much needed addition to the field of money psychology."

—Olivia Mellan, Psychologist, Author of *Money Harmony & Overcoming Overspending*

***

"This was the first book to address couples core issues and it's still the best one around. It's the only one I recommend in my book. I believe this needs to be required reading for all couples, I got so many insights personally. Money is such a sensitive issue in most relationships this should be read even before problems arise."

—Barbara Stanney, Author of *Prince Charming Isn't Coming: How Women Get Smart About Money*

Books by Victoria F. Collins

Couples and Money
A Couples' Guide for the New Millennium

Divorce and Money

Smart Ways to Save Money Before and After Divorce

Your Next Fifty Years,
A New Way to Look at How, When and Whether to Retire

Couples

MONEY

Couples *and* Money

A Couples' Guide Updated for the New Millennium

Victoria F. Collins, Ph.D., CFP

with Suzanne Blair Brown

Foreword by Rennie Gabriel

Gabriel Publications

COUPLES AND MONEY

For information address:
Gabriel Publications
5189 Gaviota Ave.
Encino, CA 914236-1428 U.S.A.
email: renniecoach@earthlink.net
http://www.financial-coach.com

10 9 8 7 6 5 4 3 2 1 pbk

Bantam hardcover edition published March 1990
Bantam paperback rack edition March 1992

In association with Meridian House 1997

ISBN 1-891689-98-3

Typography: Synergistic Data Systems
Cover by Marc Leunis, Leunis, Inc.

PRINTED IN THE UNITED STATES OF AMERICA

Contents

Acknowledgments

It's true that no book is ever written solely by the person called the author. As you read this book, I would like you to be aware of the many exceptional people who played a part in making it happen. My special thanks go to:

First and foremost, Suzanne Blair Brown, who gave life to my thoughts, ideas, theories, and words. Thanks go also to Mary Claire Blakeman, herself a talented writer, and our 'right hand' throughout the entire project. As 'in-house' editor and director of research, she integrated vast amounts of information, teased out elusive concepts, and brought focus and clarity to all.

Rennie Gabriel, who has been the catalyst for the new edition of this book. His support, patience, encouragement and professionalism have meant so much.

Joe Dominguez and Vicki Robin who co-authored the best seller, *Your Money or Your Life*, which was an inspiration to me. It is as significant and insightful a book on the subject that you'll ever find.

Olivia Mellan, one of the most skillful marriage and family counselors in the country, has been a good friend and shared her expertise in helping us analyze what really goes on with couples and money.

My friends and associates at Keller, Coad & Collins, with special thanks to Christine Velez, whose help has been invaluable in so many ways—and for so many years.

David, my husband, mentor, sounding board, and closest friend. His perceptive insights, constructive ideas, and never-ending encouragement were true gifts to me personally and to the completion of this book.

Deep appreciation goes also to my mother and dad, who taught me the money values that have served me so well.

Finally, warmest thanks go to another very special group of people: the clients and couples I interviewed who shared their experiences openly and honestly so that this book could be written. I've learned so much from them about how to meet the challenge of making money and relationships work in today's world.

Foreword

I t's an honor and a thrill to write the foreword for this book. Long before I met Victoria Collins, I had been using exercises from her book in my UCLA classes, recommending her book in my workshops and suggesting it to couples that I met with individually.

When I first read *Couples and Money*, it became instantly obvious how special it was. It addresses the emotional aspects that get in the way of couples speaking and working on their money. It offers practical exercises with the education that couples need to stop fighting and creatively realize their financial goals.

Couples and Money was first published by Bantam Books and sold over 20,000 copies. It was recommended by Consumer Credit Counseling Services, which has over 1200 offices across the United States. This non-profit organization offers education and free financial counseling to individuals and couples who get into money or credit problems.

Since 1990 this book has assisted tens of thousands of couples to communicate more effectively when discussing money. Arguing over money is the leading cause of divorce in this country. Sex, child-rearing and fidelity are not the primary sources of conflict—differing opinions and behaviors about money are the primary cause. Through this book, people can see how their past impacts their future. They can work on exercises which create blame-free conversations. It allows couples to team up to build a road of financial prosperity and financial independence.

This new, revised edition has been updated for the new millennium. Victoria devoted months researching current struggles pertaining to financial survival. Besides offering solutions to old struggles, it also solves new concerns. In addition, I took the liberty of adding footnotes. These, along with the glossary I've added, provide definitions for terms with which some people may not be familiar—and a simple thing such as a definition of a word can open up a world of new understanding! Any comments about them should be referred to me, as the opinions expressed in the glossary are mine, and not Victoria's.

Since Victoria wrote the original edition of this book in 1989, her practice has changed enormously. At that time, she worked with many couples to resolve the financial conflicts which frequently come up in relationships. She currently enjoys an excellent reputation as an investment manager and partner in the Irvine, California firm of Keller, Coad & Collins, which manages well over $400 million. She is frequently featured on TV, radio and in national publications.

—**Rennie Gabriel, CLU, CFP**
President, The Financial Coach, Inc.

Rennie is a UCLA Instructor, author, publisher, former President for the Northern Los Angeles chapter of the International Association for Financial Planning (IAPP), past member of the national finance committee for the Employee Assistance Professionals Association (EAPA), past board member of the Apartment Association, listed in Who's Who in Finance and Industry, and selected Man of the Year by the American Biographical Institute.

Rennie holds public workshops in Los Angeles and works with Fortune 500 corporations in the areas of business development, productivity and time management. The testimonial letters he receives demonstrate the power of his work. A highly effective business coach, his humor creates presentations which are a superb balance of inspiration and immediately usable practical tools. He can be reached at (818) 906-2147, or by email: renniecoach@earthlink.net.

Love: What's Money Got To Do With it?

Money can get in the way of love, even in the most romantic, compatible relationships. Of all the intimacies you share, the sharing of money sparks the most arguments, kindles the most resentments, and creates the most confusion. From what I've seen, it also causes the most divorces.

Things don't necessarily get easier as you get richer. Usually, the stakes just get higher and the problems more baffling. Financial life, especially when it enters the bedroom, can be harder to figure out than quantum physics, harder to talk about than sex.

Most of us dive into relationships or marriages utterly unprepared. Of course, it used to be easier. There was a time when the rules were straightforward: men worked and earned the money; women stayed home and spent it.

As traditional male-female relationship structures go the way of penny candy and nickel Cokes, couples, whether married or not, are left to figure out the touchy topic of domestic finance on their own. Who will pay for what? How will joint incomes be shared? Who will pay to support the kids from previous marriages? How will we manage the paperwork, the investments and all those insidious daily financial decisions when our habits are so different? Why do we never seem to have enough money? Where does it all go?

1

There's much more to family financial life than tracking the dollars earned, saved, and spent. In addition to any financial portfolio either partner may have—stocks, bonds, properties, and/or cash—each of them brings to the new relationship a psychological portfolio of beliefs, attitudes, memories, biases, fears, and needs.

Considering the inadequate instructions about money management that most of us were given, trying to merge *both* portfolios without guidance is like trying to figure out an elaborate computer program without the manual.

And the economic environment is doing little to make the business of love work more smoothly. Just knowing all you need to know, and doing all you need to do, add a mega-dose of stress to normal, daily financial life.

Most couples today are navigating life with two careers or are attempting to reconcile traditional husband and wife roles in these nontraditional postfeminist times. They're riding the roller-coaster fluctuations in the market and living through sudden ascents from rags to riches and, just as often, sudden descents from riches to rags.

It's hardly surprising that most couples, at some point, fight about money. Of all modern sources of irritation, money is the most constant. It presents itself as an issue every time you open your mail or go for your wallet to pay for lunch.

From my unique vantage point as a Certified Financial Planner with a Ph.D. in psychology, I have listened to countless couples tell me their stories, both of success and of woe.

Maybe he likes to spend money, while she squirrels away every spare nickel; or she loves daredevil market risks and he longs for the safety of a CD.* One makes financial decisions on the spot, while the other mulls them over for weeks; or one is a fiend for tracking every penny on the computer, while the other keeps receipts wadded up in a shoe box.

I believe that it's not only what you see on the balance sheets,** but also the psychological dynamics that lie between the balance

---

* CD – Certificate of Deposit.
** balance sheet – the form which lists everything an individual or couple own, and everything they owe.

sheets, that make the difference between a marriage or partnership that works and one that doesn't.

As a financial planner, I was schooled in numbers and logic—skills that suggested few protocols that could help these couples stop fighting about money. As a psychologist, I knew that communication skills and what we know about the psychology of relationships would play an important part.

To help others, I had to think back on my own transitions, to explore my own experiences in love and money.

I married at nineteen and accepted, with little question, my traditional role of wife and homemaker. My husband earned the money; I managed it. We had few resources, but we tackled everything as a joint project, from rearing children to remodeling homes.

As the years passed, Bob's business thrived and my work as a college professor became recognized. Financial success seemed to arrive all at once. Our relationship changed—subtly at first and then unmistakably. The lean years of working together toward mutual goals were over. My husband's fast-paced corporate world with its deals, power, money and attractive women held far more allure. As we began living a more luxurious life-style, it felt as though we were also living very separate lives.

After the marriage ended, I spent late nights ruminating: What had gone wrong? All the usual failures came to mind. One theme with variations kept playing: If I earned more, would he have thought my work more worthwhile? Would I have been more important to him? Would money have bought me more 'say' in our relationship? Could money have saved it?

These questions never would have occurred to women in my mother's generation. Something very different was happening in today's love/money relationships, and I was a part of that.

The last thing I had expected was to be a single mother of two at the age of forty.

Money relationships continued to perplex me. I began to distance myself from the domain of 'love' as I knew it in my marriage, and took to the world of business with wholehearted zeal. As I joined the mainstream of singles life as a financially independent woman, there were no guidelines—just a million questions.

How would I handle the finances of divorce? When I went on dates, who would pay? When I dated men who had more money than I, how could I keep my power? When I dated men with less money, would their masculinity be threatened?

So the transition began—from the traditional pursuits of motherhood and teaching to the fast-paced field of finance and planning. And when I married for the second time, it was under vastly different circumstances.

David and I are both busy professionals. His business and my financial-planning practice are common interests we've shared—from board room to bedroom.

Neither of us was 'trained' for the challenges we faced in the early years: how to split expenses; how to maintain separate property and still have mutual financial goals; how to handle a commuter marriage between my home in northern California and his in southern California; how to rebuild trust; and, yes, how to accept our different attitudes and habits.

How did we make it work? I was aware that even though we loved each other very much, money issues could undermine what we had and what we were trying to build. These issues cropped up in the most trifling matters (who would pay the gardener) as well as in major decisions (whose assets would we use to make large real estate investments).

The differences showed up in our values, priorities, and goals. We laughed about them, talked about them, and yes, we argued about them on occasion.

Over the last few years, since we started what's been a very happy partnership, David and I realized the importance of creating ground rules for our financial relationship that would meet our needs as individuals and as a couple. I knew that what we learned together about creating a successful, albeit complex, marriage could help other couples who were caught in the same traps.

To help my clients I developed a system for reconciling financial and psychological portfolios, to make them a single enterprise in what is an economic partnership. That system became the inspiration for and central theme of this book.

This is a book about the men and women I've seen in my practice, as well as those who were part of a two-year research project in which I interviewed more than eighty couples. They confided in me their past experiences with money, their power struggles, fights, values, dreams, and transitions. They described the subjects of their major debacles and minor squabbles.

In order to protect confidentiality, I have changed all names and created composite characters to illustrate the common financial 'types' I've met.

I wrote this book to help these couples, and to help you understand financial tensions, resolve disputes, and find prosperity in both love and money.

To achieve those desired ends requires more than just attentive reading. This book is divided into two parts. Part I is about the psychology of money behavior and what happens when we bring our beliefs, biases and quirks into a relationship. Part II answers the question: Now that we know why we are the way we are, how can we resolve our money differences and get on with the far more pleasurable business of love?

From time to time I will ask you to do some exercises and fill out questionnaires. These exercises have been carefully designed to get you to actively investigate (and, if necessary, change) your present love/money dynamics. At times it may be difficult to take pencil in hand and answer questions. It may be even more difficult to discuss the results with your mate. But if you feel resistance, it may be because something important has been touched upon.

This book is a financial management primer which I hope will get you well on your way. I must emphasize, however, that it won't be a cure-all for serious emotional or financial troubles. In some instances you will need the support of a Certified Financial Planner or a licensed therapist. There are many fine professionals in both fields and I wholeheartedly encourage you to work with them.

I have watched many couples transform the quality of their relationships and the shape of their finances. In order to have rich relationships, robust enough to survive these turbulent times as we greet the new millennium, we need to have a clear understanding of where we have been and where we are going.

PART ONE

How Did We Get Here?

Chapter ONE

Money Messages from the Past

*Truth #1: When love and money meet,
the past is always present.*

"**W**e make plenty of money," said Cory. "But God only knows what happens to it after it hits our bank accounts."

It was Cory and Sheila's first financial-planning appointment. He was an attorney, tall, sandy-blond, and striking, with a rugged, just-off-the-football field look. The contrast with his wife, Sheila, who arrived primly clad in navy-blue dress and pearls, was staggering.

From the outset it was hard for me to get a word into the conversation. Cory launched into a monologue, outlining for me in a thick New York accent a picture of their income, expenses, needs, and financial backgrounds. With each financial revelation he grew more irritable, and anger welled up in his voice until he was nearly shouting.

"We don't have a clue how much it costs us to live," he complained. "Our books are a mess. We have a lot of stocks, but we don't even keep track of how those investments are doing. The rest of our assets are in money market accounts*—safe, but very little return. We've avoided doing anything more aggressive. Money is just beyond our control, which is why we've come to you."

He hardly glanced at Sheila, who sat beside him for the first half hour of our meeting in unbroken silence. At first I interpreted her incessant gazing around my office and shifting in her chair as lack of interest. Only her fingernail-biting hinted at an underlying tension beneath the apparent boredom.

A quick reading of their tax returns proved of little help in unraveling the problem. Cory brought home sizable sums from his law practice, and Sheila earned a decent salary as an office manager who supervised a dozen employees. She had also received a hefty inheritance from her mother's estate. They should have been living comfortably on that income—but living well they were not.

"We aren't total spendthrifts," Sheila blurted, breaking her long silence abruptly. "I mean, going shopping at the mall isn't our idea of cultural entertainment. We just need a little investment advice, that's all. Cory likes to do this financial hardship routine, but we do just fine. I hope we're not going to get into a big long dissertation on every dime we make or spend. If so, I'd rather leave right now."

"Don't start that again here, Sheila, for God's sake," Cory retorted. "You know damn well what kind of lousy shape we're in."

What Are Hidden Investments?

When I first became a Certified Financial Planner I naively assumed that cases like Cory and Sheila's could be easily solved. The detective work would involve finding the right financial plan: sound cash-flow management system, well-balanced stock portfolio, efficient insurance policies, and the like. Theirs should have been an open-and-shut textbook case in which sound planning led to successful financial results (read: more money). More money leads to happiness. Right? Wrong.

---

* Money Market Account – a stock brokerage account similar to a standard savings account at a bank. Generally pays higher interest and can allow check writing privileges.

Over the years, I've seen too many of my best-laid financial plans fail or get shelved, like any other unfinished household project.

Everything I read in the press and hear from my colleagues confirms what I am seeing in my own office. Couples are fighting more about money now than ever before—and those fights are raging among the rich as well as the poor.

Fortunately, I had my background as a psychologist to draw upon. And as I took a deeper look into the money woes of couples like Cory and Sheila, it dawned on me how much more there was to money—and to relationships surrounding money—than could be seen on a balance sheet.

I realized that my clients brought with them two portfolios. One, the financial, contained their stocks and bonds, net worth[*] and cash flow statements[**]—all the bottom-line information that can be quantified on paper. The other, what I call the 'psychological portfolio,' is filled with the unconscious beliefs, emotions, feelings, fears, superstitions and experiences symbolically linked to money.

This portfolio of psychologically-based money attitudes has as much to do with the financial well-being or woe of a couple as the facts and figures in a financial portfolio.[***]

Besides stocks and certificates of deposit, I would have to find out what other investments were at work in love/money partnerships, what unconscious beliefs had been bought and traded during the course of each partner's financial life.

These weren't easy questions to broach. To really serve my clients, I'd have to broaden the scope of financial planning as we know it. My goal became to clarify for people not only how their money works but what that money means to them.

The real mission of financial planning, for me, is to help couples become successful with their money and with each other. That

---

[*] net worth – the amount of money left over if you added up everything you own and subtracted everything you owe.

[**] cash flow statement – a method of presentation which shows money that has come in and shows where it has been spent.

[***] portfolio – someone's investment holdings as a group; can include stocks, bonds, mutual funds, real estate and other businesses owned.

means bringing clarity and balance to both the financial and psychological portfolios.

To find out why money gets in the way of love, we start by looking at the seeds of what makes people different from one another. In other words, we begin by looking into the past. In each individual's personal money history we discover the first holdings of the psychological portfolio: Hidden Investments—the attitudes, memories, and money messages internalized over a lifetime.

Everyone invests in money beliefs. Like an investment made with real dollars, Hidden Investments in money attitudes are resources you wager in anticipation of getting something of greater value in return. You buy into your money beliefs hoping they'll lead you to a happier and more secure life. That doesn't always happen.

When hidden from consciousness, like clothes left unworn too long in a closet, those investments grow obsolete. They become inconsistent with economic realities and emotional needs. They can actually undermine the well-being you thought they would guarantee.

If you've ever found yourself in a rage about some trivial matter that vaguely reminded you of a sour experience in the past—or if you've found yourself fighting for some money ethic you didn't really believe in and sounding eerily like one of your parents—those were your Hidden Investments at work.

Hidden Investments are core beliefs, both useful and harmful, accumulated through the natural course of learning. They come into play every time you sell a house, buy a bag of groceries, or give your child a few coins for a candy bar. And Hidden Investments are in the middle of the fray each time you have money differences with your mate.

They are inherited from parents and peers, absorbed from the media, the religious environment and the society around you. Hidden Investments are reinforced by your own positive and negative experiences with money, and determine forever after how you will react when subjects such as risk, checkbooks, investments and spending arise.

In the case of Sheila and Cory, Hidden Investments were evidently at work beneath the surface of two successful careers. Why would a competent woman like Sheila, sharp enough to run an entire office for others, become suddenly inept with her own money? Why was money so hard for her to talk about? What was Cory so angry about? Why did relatively minor, solvable money difficulties appear so enormous?

And what about the sniping repartee they conducted in my office? I could only assume it was mild compared to the fights they were probably having at home.

With Cory and Sheila's permission, we began looking at the Hidden Investments that each of them, unknowingly, brought with them to our session. We began with their earliest money memories.

"My father not only didn't like to spend his own money, he didn't want anyone else to spend money either," reflected Cory. "He was judgmental, domineering, and cheap. Money was the central focus of all effort in our family. Every decision came down to one thing: How much is it going to cost?

"When we were kids we all had to work at Dad's gas station. It didn't build a strong family bond. He was tyrannical and I remember in those days thinking of money as my passport to independence. Being free from my father was something I longed for."

"Do you see anything about your money relationship with Sheila that reminds you of your father?" I asked.

"God, no!" Cory fired back. "I swore I'd never be like him."

When I didn't respond, giving Cory time to cool down, he paused. A few moments later he said, "Come to think of it, I do tend to ride her over our finances, because Sheila doesn't seem to care one way or the other... But most of what I do is purposely designed so I won't be like him."

"In what ways do you ensure you aren't like him?" I ventured.

"I remember when he died and the size of his estate became known, I was shocked. He had amassed a lot of money, which is amazing considering he just ran a gas station. I remember thinking to myself how much of life he had wasted. I don't think he had any fun at all. It became a driving ambition of mine to enjoy money, and not to die with piles of money stashed somewhere."

"So what are you doing about it? Are you spending what you have?"

"It's almost like that penurious* part of him still lives in me, even though I rebel against it. I don't want to watch every cent in my pocket like he did, but my being so casual and inattentive helped Sheila and me get into the bind we're in. The same time, it's really hard to spend money. I remember hating our vacation in Europe because I felt awful every time I had to pay those high prices for food and hotels. I guess I'm just always tense about it, and I know that tension causes a lot of my fights with Sheila."

"What about your background with money?" I asked Sheila.

"You know, when you asked us that at first I couldn't recollect one concrete thing about money in our family. It was never discussed—ever. My mother had money from her family and my dad never had any, and I think that was a real problem for them. So we just never talked about it and pretended Dad was a big breadwinner."

"Were there tensions about money?" I asked.

"Tensions! Lord, yes. My parents never fought about it openly. But we all knew when it was tax time. My father would rant and rave during the two weeks it took him to prepare the returns. I remember one night my mom tried to take his mind off the IRS by serving us a huge turkey dinner. Friends and relatives had joined us. The turkey was an obvious extravagance and a real treat. But it turned out really tough and stringy. We all began to laugh about it. My father suddenly blew up and threw the carving knife at the turkey. As grease went splattering all over us, I remember thinking, if this is what money does to adults—I don't want any part of it."

"If money wasn't talked about in your family, how do you manage to discuss it with Cory?" I queried.

"We don't. I loathe having anything to do with the subject. Nothing ruins a dinner out for me faster than having people fight over the check and pull out money. I get instantly nauseous."

"Turkey-dinner phobia," I said, smiling.

"Guess so," Sheila laughed. "I don't like any financial details. I take the price tags off of groceries before I put them in the refrigerator. You shouldn't have to be reminded about money every time you make yourself a tuna salad sandwich."

---

* penurious – extremely stingy

In our subsequent meetings, I explained to Sheila and Cory the concept of Hidden Investments. Both had brought into their financial marriage some strong, negative, and highly charged beliefs and values regarding money. Those odious memories had become an emotional obstacle course, keeping them stumbling and arguing through what could have been a prosperous relationship.

In spite of his quest for independence from his father, the image of a stern and miserly patriarch haunted Cory, sending him into fits of fury over trifles and keeping him purposefully vague about money.

Sheila spent all her energy dodging money discussions altogether. From her mother she learned that open dialogue about money can reveal horrible hidden truths and endanger marriages. Even the simplest discussions about light bills and dinner checks were magnified in her mind as possibly explosive confrontations.

The result of these complex overlapping Hidden Investments lay before me in the form of an utterly inefficient financial portfolio. Yet organizing the checkbooks and investment statements would be a cinch compared with dealing with the deeper, more fundamental emotional investments at hand.

It isn't my intention to throw light on every dark little corner of the psyche. If couples like Sheila and Cory are to quit using money to abuse each other, however, they must engage in a workable discussion about what money has meant to them in the past—and what it means now.

If they can trace for themselves the path upon which they arrived at their present money personalities, they might become more compassionate partners. Eventually, the Hidden Investments that no longer serve them will disappear.

Spheres of Money Influence

I often illustrate the different levels of Hidden Investments by using concentric circles to show the different spheres of money influence. The model helped Sheila and Cory to fashion a more productive dialogue about money. Perhaps it will help you, too.

See the diagram on the next page.

The innermost sphere reflects the beliefs in which you invest as children—your earliest views on money, power, and relationships.

Spheres of Money Influence

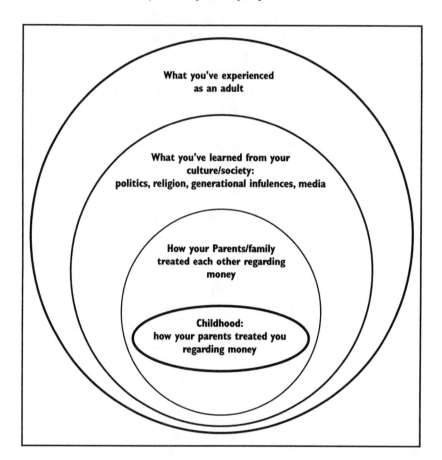

The spheres extend outward to include all other environmental influences.

Moving from the middle of the circle toward the exterior rings, the influences become more conscious and more amenable to change. The unconscious core beliefs nearest to the center are the most stubborn and impervious to change. This will become clearer as we take a look at the individual influences that determine how you behave with money today.

Childhood and Money Messages from the Cradle

I believe that by the age of twelve your core money attitudes and values have been formed. What happens from then on, from a psychological point of view, is simply padding and proof.

Your financial life from cradle to junior high school is worth a serious second look.

What's the worst advice your mother and father ever gave you? Was it that you should forgo your talents in the arts and find a 'real' job? That you should save all your money for a rainy day? That you should never trust a man—or a woman—when it comes to money?

Parental advice about money, usually well intended, was the most influential information you ever got on the subject. In the eyes of the child you were, it wasn't just a fallible human's opinion of how the world works. The messages you heard in those heart-to-heart talks with Mom and Dad were believed more deeply than if they'd been handed down from God on tablets of stone. I will never forget a client I had many years ago who gave up a promising singing career just after her first album had hit the national charts. Only later did she realize the truth about her choice. It all went back to something her mother often told her: "No man wants to marry a woman who makes more money than he does. A wife should keep her place."

When your parents gave you advice about money, did you ever stop to consider the source? How well did they do in love? With money? How much of what they said was true? And even if it were true for them, how relevant is it to your present life? These questions bring to mind an old joke: Two goldfish were swimming in their bowl, contemplating the nature of existence. When it came to the question of a higher order, one fish asked the other, "If there's no God, then who changed the water?"

As children we're like those goldfish. For lack of complete information about the way the world works, we assign authority—even divinity—to the most powerful people around: parents.

Often what was said about money was not reflected in what was done about it. Parents, like the rest of humanity, are notoriously inconsistent. They may have extolled the virtue of saving, even while they continued to overspend.

To make matters still more complex, most of your money beliefs were handed down to you nonverbally, in the silent, unwritten etiquette of the domestic financial life you observed. Perhaps money was treated with sacred secrecy, only changing hands behind locked doors. Or maybe it was flaunted in public to impress others.

Not only do we unconsciously emulate our parents, but many people go through their adult lives trying to live up to the financial laws and standards they were taught as ten-year-olds. It doesn't matter if those standards are achievable. In many cases it doesn't matter if those parents are even still alive.

When Jack came home, the fairy tale goes, he gave his mother the beans he'd received in payment for selling the family cow. She was furious. To show him what she thought of the deal, she threw the beans out in the garden and made poor Jack go to bed without dinner. Fortunately for Jack, the beans were magic. A giant beanstalk grew. Jack climbed it, and in that land above the clouds he defeated an angry giant, made off with his money, captured a hen that laid golden eggs, and was able to buy his mother a whole herd of cattle.

Whether we know it or not, there is some Jack in most of us. The desire to please our parents and bring home that all-profitable hen is nearly universal.

A wealthy businesswoman I once knew, for example, suffered a vague foreboding guilt whenever she made a major purchase. That guilt was driving her particularly crazy the evening before she closed escrow on a new home in an up-scale San Francisco neighborhood. We analyzed and reanalyzed the figures: It was a great investment which she could easily afford. She kept coming back to the thought, however, that her parents would think it was too extravagant.

Much of what was learned from parents who grew up in a far different socioeconomic age begs to be re-evaluated in light of today's hyperactively changing world, as well as the changing needs of today's relationships.

Society: How Money Makes the World Go 'Round

Parents may have the first word on money, but it's never the final one. From your friends, from your church, and from the newspaper that hits your porch in the morning and the television that beams into your living room at night, you receive millions of culturally based money messages.

Those you adopt can become Hidden Investments, biases you take on merely because "everyone else" believes them, too. They make the helter-skelter world of money more sane.

What were some of the money messages you picked up over the cultural transmission lines? Do these sound familiar?

- Money is the root of all evil.
- Money talks.
- Living well is the best revenge.
- Put your money where your mouth is.
- Money doesn't grow on trees.
- A penny saved is a penny earned.
- A bird in the hand is worth two in the bush.
- You can never be too thin or too rich.
- What you give you will receive.
- He who dies with the most toys wins.

Clichés become clichés because they're repeated so often they solidify into hard-and-fast truth. If you lived in a small town full of people who thought exactly as you did, cut off from all media and foreign input, it's possible you might grow up completely consistent in your feelings about money.

In the real world, clichés and beliefs are at odds with one another. You're fed a steady diet of inconsistencies, blatant contradictions and lies about money:

- Earning money is good; having too much of it is bad.
- Women should find men with money, but marry only for love.

- Men should work hard to raise the standard of living of their families; but even a lot of money is never, finally, enough.

- Men should be providers, but women should be equal partners.

- Women should be successful in work, but shouldn't earn more than men.

Those Hidden Investments you adopt from the world around you break down even further. Let's take a closer look at some of those socially-based beliefs.

The Generation in Which You Came of Financial Age

The pervading sentiments of the economic times you're reared in have a lot to say about how you perceive money. Depression-era children react very differently to words like 'debt' and 'risk' than do the young professionals of the 1980s who cut their teeth on credit cards. Those who actually stood in bread lines tend to have different money fears from those raised in the age of croissants.

Sean and Kate, two clients whose families suffered miserable losses in the stock market crash of 1929, just couldn't be convinced that part of their portfolio in the 1990's should include at least some high-growth mutual funds. "We've seen what can happen," Kate said to me more than once.

The Political Landscape You Were Reared in

Political alliances can generate formidable Hidden Investments. While there are certainly rich Democrats, poor Republicans, and capitalistic Socialists, political beliefs can have remarkable effects on money beliefs.

In the 1960's an entire segment of American youth adopted the belief that making money meant selling out, and that the pursuit of wealth was morally suspect. Many a latter-day hippie has been climbing the corporate ladder with those beliefs from college days strapped on like ankle weights. Meanwhile, the college kids of the Reagan '80's applauded the pursuit of MBA's and BMW's.

The Church You Pray in and the God You Worship

Where the theology of money is concerned, religions vary widely in their teaching. On one extreme are the ascetic and fundamentalist religions that consider displays of personal wealth sinful, and hard work the only path to paradise.

On the other extreme are many of the so-called 'New Age' or 'New Thought' religions, which impart a spiritual sanction to material abundance.

The most dominant religious influence on money beliefs in this country comes from the Judeo-Christian tradition. When the *Mayflower* docked here, the Puritan ethic landed, too. Psychologist Henry Clay Lindgren writes in *Great Expectations*: "Christianity was from the very beginning a religion of the poor. It glorified poverty and was contemptuous of wealth. For example, the authors of the gospels have Jesus telling his followers that 'a camel may more easily pass through the eye of a needle than a rich man may enter the Kingdom of God.'"

The most memorable case I've seen of religiously-based Hidden Investments at work was Bob, a retired aerospace engineer who came to see me for retirement planning. Raised in a strict fundamentalist religion, he'd spent nearly his entire young life studying the Bible and praying for salvation. At the age of fifty, after a successful career and two coronary bypasses, he refused to take vacations or buy the motor home he'd always wanted. As his wife, Carla, once confided, "Bob still thinks he's going to go to hell if he has any fun."

The Media's Message

Just as they can get us to buy Pepsi and Ty-D-Bol, the media—radio, television, magazines and newspapers—give us enough money messages to short-circuit the average mind. And their money thinking is wildly inconsistent.

The popular press, as a group, has long been suspicious of vast displays of wealth. As the newspaper giant Joseph Pulitzer once said, the purpose of the press is to "comfort the afflicted and afflict the comfortable." The media have been subjecting the comfortable to an intense scrutiny of values and practices ever since.

Yet, while they cast the rich as morally dubious with one stroke of the pen, they glorify them with the next. The rich live in the public mind as demigods—some good, some evil, but gods nonetheless. We see their faces plastered all over the covers of tabloids. We pore over the photographs of their homes and yachts. We devour stories of their lavish lifestyles.

Nowhere has this adulation been practiced more guilelessly than on television's *Lifestyles of the Rich and Famous*. It's easy to think those chosen few who frolic in Rolls-Royces, globe-trot from Bali to Brazil, and cavort in houses the size of hotels live in an endless summer of bliss. Every once in a while, tales of nasty divorces, scandalous palimony suits, or Dantesque descents into drinking and drugs momentarily shatter the illusion that money equals love equals happiness. But the belief that once we are very rich we will be very content prevails in the public mind—in spite of all evidence to the contrary.

Messages from the Recent Past

The most obvious layer of money beliefs comes from the financial trials and errors of your own past. Taken to extremes, however, financial choices that worked once are hailed as the 'Only Conceivable Choice' to make forever after. Those that didn't pan out are catalogued under 'Terrible Ideas' to be fervently avoided. (To paraphrase a thought from Mark Twain: A cat that sits down on a hot stove will never sit on a hot stove again . . . nor will it ever sit on a cold one.)

By the same token, traumatic financial experiences involving losses, divorces, business failures, and debts create a cache of Hidden Investments that may or may not be openly recognized between mates. Once traumatized by an experience, people tend to be wary of circumstances that even resemble it.

The most common arenas for this are second marriages and second businesses.

Phil is a good example. Burned by a messy divorce in which he lost most of what he'd earned in his lifetime, he treated his new wife, Angela, with miserly suspicion. If she went to the store to buy ice cream, he grabbed the receipt and studied it. He monitored her checkbook and made her account for every nickel. If Phil had recognized and divested himself of these Hidden Investments, his second wife might have had a chance. Instead, the marriage didn't last out the year. But he remained true to his purpose: "never to be taken to the cleaners by a woman again."

The Hidden Investments gleaned from the trials and errors of adult life are usually good guidelines for future choices. However, when undue attention is paid to these negative influences, both finances and marriages suffer for—rather than profit from—the mistakes of the past.

Selective Money Memories

Selective money memories not only keep the past Hidden Investments alive, but also help us create new ones every day.

Have you ever found yourself saying to your partner, "I always have to be the responsible one and pay the bills," even when he is responsible sometimes. Or do you let accusations fly, such as "You never write down your checks," even though sometimes she does?

You aren't lying. You are just remembering events selectively. It's a complex psychological process called selective memory—a kind of built-in editor of experience. Simply stated, you tend to call to mind all the memories that support your opinion and to omit those that don't.

When you remember only part of the story, you start to believe that only the part you recall is true. No other information is allowed into the system to challenge the memory. It would force you to re-examine your version of reality, and there's almost nothing the human mind dislikes more.

Have you ever noticed that when you're shopping for a new car and are interested in one kind, you see it everywhere? Likewise, once your distorted version of a story is in place, you'll find supporting evidence for it everywhere. The evidence mounts. That's how selective memory reinforces our Hidden Investments.

So, if you believe your mate is extravagant, you'll only notice the Italian shoes, French sunglasses and Danish cheese he likes to buy. All the times he actually saves money never register. On the other hand, if you think your loved one really is a cheapskate, you focus on the sale-rack clothes and fast-food dinner dates while ignoring the conscientious selection of a good stereo or the comfortable life you enjoy because of diligent saving.

The problem with a selective money memory is that it gives us a distorted picture of reality. If your memory tells you that your mate 'always' spends too much, you can't tell if he or she is really overspending.

Hidden Investments: A Personal Inventory

You won't ever get rid of all your Hidden Investments. They're a part of who you are. They help you to make sense out of all the information you receive. But you can expose them to the light of day. Squarely facing long-buried beliefs means knowing yourself in an intimate way. By understanding where your money habits, attitudes, and quirks come from, you are free to choose: keep them or toss them out with yesterday's newspaper. Keeping those beliefs means taking responsibility for them, instead of constantly pointing the finger at your partner.

I devised a short inventory to uncover and disclose Hidden Investments. In my research and practice, I have given this questionnaire to hundreds of individuals over the years. All report learning something new about themselves and their partners.

Take a moment to ask yourself these questions. Write down your responses. Ask your partner to do the same.

1. What was my mother's role concerning finances? How is my role like hers?

2. What was my father's role concerning finances? How is my role like his?

3. As a child, did I think I was rich, poor, or middle class? How do the feelings I had then affect my perception of money now?

4. What were the main messages my parents gave me regarding money? How closely do I follow them—or how strongly do I rebel against them—today?

5. What are the money traumas I've experienced? What lessons did I learn from them? How have those lessons altered the way I deal with money now?

6. What big money successes have I had? What lessons did I learn? How have those lessons altered the way I deal with money now?

7. What is my greatest fear regarding money?

8. In thinking about all the things I do (or could do) with money, what makes me the most uncomfortable? What gives me the greatest pleasure?

9. Are my partner and I well matched in money values? On what do we agree? Disagree?

10. In what generation did I 'come of age' financially?

11. Now, when I think of money, I see it as _____.

12. When it comes to being rich, I always pictured myself as _____ in the movie _____.
    When I think of being poor, I picture myself as _____ in the movie _____.

13. At coffee breaks my colleagues always have this to say about money: _____.

14. The last time I trusted someone with money I _____.

Now ask yourself: Are the beliefs and fears reflected in my answers serving me in my present circumstances? Which ones will I hold on to? Which ones should have been discarded long ago? And how are these attitudes helping or hindering my love relationship?

One couple, Cory and Sheila, completed their questionnaire and came back to me excited. For the first time in their relationship, Cory accepted that Sheila's anxiety was real for her. He stopped seeing her as 'silly' and began watching for signals of her money discomfort. With new sensitivity they developed their own personal code. A light touch of the hand when the subject of money came up meant "I know this is awkward for you and I understand." When they ate out, Sheila's after-dinner trip to the restroom became the ideal time to pay the dinner check.

Sheila began to understand Cory's tensions about having and spending money. Whenever she saw his temper begin to flare, she could tell he was feeling those old anxieties he had learned from his father. The question "How's your dad?" meant "I understand and I'm here to listen."

When love and money meet, the past is always present, in some form. Think about your own Hidden Investments. Decide which ones really are the sources of your current money problems. Discuss with your partner how an understanding of each other's past beliefs and experiences might help you ease current tensions. Knowing where the financial portfolio ends, and the psychological portfolio begins means knowing yourselves financially in a new and intimate way. Still, uncovering your Hidden Investments is only the first step. There's more work to be done.

Chapter TWO

Men, Women, and the Money Games They Play

*Truth #2: The battle between the sexes has
no place between the balance sheets.*

The year I met them was a heady time for Roy and Cecilia. A major Hollywood production company had optioned Roy's screenplay. Cecilia, a smoldering Peruvian beauty, was gaining clout as a stage actress.

They impressed me as a quintessentially modern couple. They had lived together for years and had no marriage plans. Their financial arrangements too, had a contemporary twist. Every individually made dollar was kept separate until the couple came together with checkbooks once a month to pay bills.

"Things are just going so well the way they are," Cecilia told me then. "We're both working and, for a change, earning more than enough to live on. If we keep it going we'll be out of debt in a year. We're even thinking about buying a house—one of those little cottages in the Hollywood hills. What do you think?"

I followed their progress over the next few years through mutual friends. The dream house never materialized. A baby daughter did, however. When they came to see me for a new financial plan, I could tell trouble was brewing.

The arrival of little Melinda brought with it a wholesale restructuring of their relationship. Along with changing diapers, Cecilia and Roy found themselves in the throes of dramatically changing roles. Cecilia stayed home with the baby. Roy found himself the sole breadwinner for the first time.

"We're broke," Roy said, his usual veneer of self-confidence wearing thin. "The studio didn't promote the movie and it flopped—resoundingly. Needless to say, no one's rushing in with any new offers. That's how the screenwriting business goes. Cut one big deal and you're everyone's buddy. One bad movie, and you're a stray dog everyone feels sorry for but no one wants to take in.

"All of a sudden I have a stay-at-home wife, a new baby, and a stack of overdue bills. Cecilia offered to find part-time work. I just couldn't stand the idea of her hustling for parts in soap commercials. I'm going to make it. If I'm going to be the man in this family, I want to support us."

"I love to work," Cecilia chimed in, snuggling Melinda. "But I love being at home to take care of the baby too.

"What's amazing, as far as money goes, is the changes between Roy and me," she continued. "Everything used to be pretty clear-cut and equal. Now that he makes all the income, my whole perception of money—what I can and can't spend it on—has changed. Now it's his domain, under his control. I find myself asking if it's okay to buy things. My God, our relationship is reminding me so much of my mother and father's, it's frightening."

The New Sexual Politics of Money

Cecilia's dilemma is becoming the norm today as creative and independent women struggle to find a balance between career and motherhood. While Roy felt the need to flex his muscles as the family breadwinner, Cecilia chafed at the loss of her former financial power.

In the 1950's television show *Leave It to Beaver,* young Beaver Cleaver came home to a family where financial relationships between the sexes were homogeneous and tidy. His father brought home the paycheck and managed the family's middle-class income with benevolent authority. Beaver's mother happily made sandwiches, took care of the house and dealt with money only on the level of cookie-jar savings and small-scale domestic finance.

While the show still plays on cable television, the idyllic money roles it portrays now seem as odd as 3-D glasses in movies and tail fins on pink Cadillacs. It's hard to imagine the Cleavers, with spic-and-span family roles intact, faring well through the social upheavals of the sixties and the economic changes we've gone through in the last two decades. It's also impossible to imagine June Cleaver identifying with Cecilia's situation—an independent woman thrust into a position of dependency.

When Sigmund Freud suggested that "anatomy is destiny," he meant that the instincts and psychological makeup of men and women would determine how they would feel, think and behave.

What Freud failed to predict were the effects of massive sociological change. From his drawing room in Victorian Austria, I doubt he ever dreamed women would one day take to the board rooms, and that men would stay home, baby-wipes in hand, wrestling squirming infants to the mat.

The rules of the game are no longer straightforward. The fact is, it's hard to tell if there are any rules.

The male-as-provider and female-as-nurturer division of labor, which your parents probably took for granted, will be a luxury (or an oddity) to your grandchildren—if it even exists in their day. Yet the deep psychological patterning of those roles won't easily disappear, no matter what happens in the economy.

The very act of being together as men and women seems to exert a powerful gravitational pull. Without realizing it, many couples wake up to find they've adopted the traditional marital forms and values of their parents. And, as Cecilia said to me, "It's next to impossible to make this stay-at-home lifestyle that I'm living fit with everything I've believed in the past about being a modern woman."

Our Hidden Investment in how men or women 'should be' is stubbornly embedded in our psyches. Many an ostensibly liberated man has found himself wishing for a wife more interested in cooking him a hot breakfast than in tracking the latest fluctuations of the Dow Jones index.* And more than one savvy businesswoman has confessed to me that she longs for a man who could support her in style—if she really needed him to.

Unless you are among the few able to keep their myths congruent with their real lives, the partner you wake up with looks nothing like your fantasies. Nor would you necessarily want that. Have you wondered where those Hidden Investments in gender roles come from and why they're so persistent?

Models for the male-as-provider and female-as-nurturer stereotypes are found throughout history. Those roles have been a part of this culture for 150 years, beginning in the Victorian era when, to suit the philosophy of the day, 'love' was feminized and 'business' masculinized.

It wasn't until the burgeoning postwar economy of the 1950's, however, Beaver Cleaver's heyday, that the middle and lower classes were even able to survive on a single income. Only then did the provider/nurturer roles become attainable to all. Men worshiped at the altar of business. Women closed ranks in the cult of domesticity.

The strict division of duties didn't last long. By the mid-sixties, the women's movement and other sociological, political, and economic forces dealt a crashing blow to the provider/nurturer setup as a standard for all families. Yet, the inconsistencies remain. Cecilia and Roy, and millions like them, continue to straddle contradictory self-images regarding money.

Some of those contradictions show up in mind-boggling ways. In my interviews with clients, I've observed:

- A majority of men consider themselves the providers, even when their wives work. In other words, what he earns is seen as bread and butter; what she earns is gravy. "I feel like the burden is mostly mine, even though she makes as much

---

* Dow Jones – the most frequently quoted index which has 30 household company names such as Disney, McDonalds, Coca Cola.

money as I do," said a prominent northern California stock-broker.

- Many men defend their wives' right to work. At the same time, like Roy, they don't believe women have a duty to work. That duty remains the yoke of the man. Only a minority feel the provider role should be shared equally. One man I knew had to be treated for intense depression after losing the job he had held for twenty-three years. "He was lost without an office to go to," confided his wife. "And when I offered to pitch in and help, he barked at me, 'It's my responsibility. I'll handle it.'"

- Though men have relinquished part of their provider role to their wives, they haven't taken on a proportionate amount of the nurturer role in return. The result: Either the woman does both jobs (the 'Superwoman' so touted in the press), or both spouses neglect the nurturing chores equitably—better known as "two husbands, no wife."

- More young women than ever are training for careers. But while they take their places in offices next to men, a number still believe, deep down, those jobs are only temporary. As Al-exa, a forty-year-old client, recently told me: "I love my work. When the pressure's really on, though, I fall back into think-ing, 'If my husband made more money, I wouldn't have to be in this position. It's all his fault.'"

- Women want equality and, in some cases, achieve financial superiority. Once possessing the power of the dollar, some refuse to share it—a sin men have long been accused of. Their money remains "separate" while they help themselves to half of the husband's income to cover expenses. It's a post-feminist game that psychologist Tessa Albert Warschaw has called "What's Mine Is Mine—and What's Yours Is Mine, Too."

- The pull of sex roles is so strong that even among homosex-ual couples, partners tend to polarize toward male or female money behavior. Of course, as with heterosexual couples, this observation does not apply to all same-sex couples. Philip Blumstein and Pepper Schwartz found (in *American Couples*) that only lesbian pairs sometimes escape the rigid role definitions around money found in all other types of couples.

Men, Women, and the Money Differences Between Them

As I tell many couples, when tackling these changing sexual and financial roles it's important to give yourself a break. Men and women are not, and never will be, androgynous. Discrete internal differences will always remain, no matter what professional roles are played in the outside world. You will never see your financial life through the same eyes.

The debate among psychologists, sociologists, feminists, anthropologists, biologists, and just about everyone else continues to be: How are the sexes different from each other, especially when it comes to money?

I can't resolve this very complicated issue, but I can offer personal observations based on my personal and professional experience.

Men and women deal with money differently. They perceive it, use it, speak about it, and live with it in surprisingly diverse ways. Of course, it would be ridiculous (and wrong) to even suggest 'all men' or 'all women' are exactly the same. Nevertheless, I have noticed that the sexes diverge in three areas: training, experience, and attitude.

Training: Coming of Age Financially

New techniques of parenting have come a long way toward encouraging boys and girls to be treated and trained equitably in all subjects. Yet, until the very recent past, each sex was initiated differently to the ways and means of money. The cosmic rules we learned in the schoolyard followed most of us into mainstream financial life.

"My formative years prepared me to stretch his paycheck with Tuna Surprise," said one woman about her early education in the sexual economics of marriage.

A male client once complained to me, "When I was growing up everyone always told me to be nice to girls. They forgot to tell me those same girls I was holding the gym door open for eventually would be competing with me for a job."

As they meet in bedrooms and board rooms, both men and women are finding that the rules of financial etiquette they once learned are begging for radical overhaul. Think about your own early training for a moment. How were you raised to regard your own abilities? Your autonomy? Your relationships and financial interdependency with others? Your self-worth? These key areas are worth a closer look.

How boys and girls were taught to value their abilities can be seen in how they were once taught to ride bicycles. The scenario was typical: A father watched his child on a two-wheeler for the first time. The bicycle wobbled. The child fell and began to cry.

If the child was a boy the father probably said, "Now come on, son, pick yourself up and try again. Keep your balance in the middle of the bike. Don't get scared. You can do it. Snap to it! No more tears."

If the child was a girl, the father was more inclined to say, "There, there, honey. Are you hurt? Let's go inside and fix that scraped knee. We'll try this again some other time."

Most women in marriages today were little girls who were sheltered from their own mistakes—and from putting their abilities to the test. Notice that the father trained his son using specific information: "Keep your balance in the middle of the bike." Whether learning to put the spin on a football or to read the stock pages, boys are more likely to receive logical advice than emotional strokes. Where little boys were encouraged to venture out, and get roughed up a little in the process, girls who did the same were branded tomboys.

Boys were trained, in sports and competition, to risk and prevail. Schooled in 'hard knocks,' they were praised for being rough, daring, 'all boy.' The more girlish qualities were suspect.

Girls were taught that they are fragile, vulnerable, and soft. They learned to value safety, security and relationships. What they heard about their abilities on the day the bicycle wobbled had a lot to say about how they coped with challenges and risk decades later, the day the stock market did the same thing.

Boys and girls also face different psychological tasks in developing two important human traits: autonomy and intimacy. Both of those characteristics—the ability to act independently and the ability to relate to others—influence what men and women do with money.

According to the psychologist Lillian Rubin in her book *Intimate Strangers: Men and Women Together*, boys separate psychologically from their mothers very early on in order to develop "gender identity." By age three they've already begun to be emotionally self-contained and independent. Autonomy is demanded of them by virtue of their sex. Intimacy is the lesson they will have to re-learn in the process of becoming well-rounded, mature adults. No wonder the books *Men Are from Mars, Women Are from Venus* and *Mars and Venus in the Bedroom* by John Gray have been best sellers in the '90's. He expresses the same concept in a practicable, warm and provocative manner.

Girls, according to these authors, are not forced to separate from their primary role models to find gender identity. Because they, too, are female, they can identify emotionally and psychologically with their mothers. Unlike boys, girls can remain close to their first intimate human relationship, and that sense of connection is later extended to others. Consequently, autonomy is the primary lesson they need to learn.

I'm sure you can see how those psychological predispositions show up in the way you and your partner handle money.

From what I've observed, men, in general, operate easily with the adversarial aspects of money. They can compete with others, and don't take that competition personally. The independence and separation endured as toddlers become assets in business: You don't want to be all that intimate with your boss, employees and competitors. Men learn to camouflage insecurities with an exterior calm and rationality.

Dealing with the emotional content of money, however, is a different story. Their innate 'separateness' turns interdependence, vulnerability and communication into chores.

Women share the interdependencies and ties of financial life easily. They are more inclined to voice their fears and ask about the concerns of their mates. Dollars, to them, are just pieces in the larger puzzle of life; there's no need for the rigid boundaries men draw between work and play. For women, the challenge is to become comfortable with competition in making money.

Men and women arrive at the altar of domestic finance by different psychological paths. The result, of course, is that they sometimes have a hard time understanding each other. Women see men as lone wolves in a financial wilderness, and seek to draw them close emotionally. Men see that emotionality as a liability, and have a hard time figuring out what their wives want from them.

Another difference in the financial training of boys and girls centers on the expectations projected onto each sex. Boys are taught to earn their money, to lose their fiscal innocence on paper routes and at lemonade stands. Groomed as toddlers for their future job as providers, they grow up trying to make the grade. Making the grade means earning money.

Girls, typically, are given money as a reward. Earning money is presented as an option, not an imperative for survival. The dollars they earn babysitting are treated more as gifts than as evidence of personal worth. Where boys spend childhood learning how to make it 'on the outside,' girls are trained to be nurturers first and are given provider skills as an afterthought.

Experience: Facing Up to Economic Inequity

When it comes to earning, spending, and saving money—its physical use—men and women come to the playing field with very different experience levels. Though equally capable, until the last few decades women weren't given equal access to college programs and jobs.

When push comes to shove, men and women use money differently because they possess different amounts of it. In 1996, a study showed that women earn 72 cents for every dollar a man earns. Progress has been made, but pay parity has yet to be achieved.

The economic consequences of unequal earning power and experience are obvious.

"It would take me a lot longer to recoup any losses after a bad investment," said one woman. "I keep a much tighter grip on my money than my husband. Whenever he loses money, he figures,

'What the hell . . . I'll just make it back tomorrow.' For me, making it back could take years."

Men have more earning power, and therefore more extra money to risk. They invest more, and accumulate more investment know-how. Women, with less earning power, are more aware of the wolves baying at the door. They need to be more cautious investing their resources, because those resources may not be easily replenished.

"I damn well resent the fact that, even though my boyfriend and I are equally capable and work in the same profession, he makes money more easily—and I fight for every promotion and raise," said an advertising representative.

It's a common resentment, and one of the formative issues of the women's movement. It shows up with particular ferocity in two paycheck marriages. Even in more traditional relationships, economic differences stir up trouble.

"If I started today, it would take me ten years to get the experience and knowledge about money that my husband already has," complained one housewife. "It really bothers me that he considers investing our money to be his territory alone."

Attitude: Seeing Money Through Different Eyes

When I first began noticing how differently men and women approached the process of financial planning, I grew concerned for my married clients. I asked myself, "If money means something different to males than it does to females, on what basis would they be making their joint financial decisions?"

Men and women have different attitudes about money, affecting everything from how they spend it to what drives them crazy about it.

For years I've watched clients of both sexes struggle to invent new financial identities. More men and women are shattering the confines of sexual happenstance than ever before. Still, differences in attitude and style remain. Recognizing those differences can create a window of understanding between the sexes. Let's look at some of those key areas where men and women diverge in their psychological approaches to money.

Goals

How do you measure success or fulfillment in your life?

"If my relationship is going well," say most women we talk to.

"If I've got money in the bank," say the men.

Women measure the quality of their lives according to their personal satisfaction. To many women even today, money is secondary, only important after they have a close, supportive, enriching relationship with a mate. To many businesswomen, money earned, while high on their priority list, is not the end-all. Making a contribution, being recognized for what they bring to the table, for their unique talents and having a supportive and family friendly work environment—all rank right up there with compensation packages.[*]

Fears

What are your worst money nightmares? What horrific fears have kept you up at night?

"No matter how much money I make, I have this gnawing anxiety that one day it might instantly be taken away," confided Anita, a thirty-three year old dentist.

The men I've talked to have more specific income-related fears: What if I'm injured? What if I get laid off? What if this stock takes a dive?

Both sexes worry about money. Women, however, fret about it more, especially about becoming suddenly destitute. The image of wandering the streets with her clothes in a shopping cart follows many women through successful career climbs; it's been labeled the 'bag lady nightmare.'

Men worry. too. But their fears are targeted on changes in real financial circumstances rather than on fantasies of sudden, inexplicable poverty. Their fears revolve around 'losing face' when there's no rent money, or letting down their friends and family.

---

[*] Compensation package – The full list of benefits paid to someone which could include salary, bonus, health insurance, retirement plan contributions, options to buy employer stock at a discount, and so on.

Risk

How well do you tolerate risk?

The typical male response is, "I'm willing to stretch out for that golden ring. As they say, 'No guts, no glory.'"

"I'd rather live to invest another day," countered one woman I talked to.

Long accused of being financially irresponsible, women have been found to be the most conservative investors. Their relatively short track record in the marketplace hasn't acclimated them to the ebb and flow of investment money. They treat their investment money gingerly, and are prone to glorify gains and consider losses catastrophic.

Men are more accustomed to the fluctuations of money and have a larger emotional threshold for risk. When they err—especially early on in financial life—they usually err on the side of risk folly. Fast and dangerous investments come to replace fast, dangerous cars as the ultimate test of manhood.

Self-confidence

How do you assess your financial competence?

Men appear to know it all, even when they don't. Women doubt they know it all, even when they do. Of the clients who have come to me for financial planning, men are least likely to ask questions, or to appear unsure. When they realize it's all right to let down their guard with me, a woman, they appear relieved. Their lives have depended on looking capable and in command, even when they were shaking in their shoes.

Women have had more permission to not know the answers. They ask questions, backtrack, hesitate, without fearing a blow to their self-worth. They err in underestimating or ignoring their considerable abilities.

Adviser Relationships

How do you choose and relate to your financial advisers?

"Based on their track record and performance," answered Henry, a retired management consultant.

"By how they relate to me, how attentive they are to my concerns, and whether I can trust them," said Sally, his wife.

Men traditionally don't mix business and pleasure in relationships with their advisers. For women, a sense of close relationship is essential. Women look for affiliation and trust in their advisers. They take the process personally. Not 'liking' an adviser can end the relationship. Men evaluate their advisers on technical merits such as credentials, how well they sell their services, and the bottom line they offer.

Decision Making

On what basis do you make financial decisions?

Women make choices for their money based on a combination of linear reasoning and intuition, with intuition and 'feeling' leading the way. Most proceed only if they trust their adviser, only if the choice 'feels' right.

Men are a different story. Sometimes they make their decisions by reasoning through the facts. Just as often, they stake their money on tips they get from friends. Many of the money moves that have made great American fortunes came from something one of the guys said on the golf course.

Attribution

When something goes wrong, whom do you blame? When something goes right, whom do you congratulate?

Attribution, in psychology, is the manner in which individuals relate consequences to causes. Many men attribute positive consequences to their own ability ("I'm glad I saw that opportunity"); negative consequences to outside circumstances ("That damned stockbroker!"). Many women tend to attribute positive results to good luck or to their adviser's good auspices ("Can you believe the stock went up so high?"); negative consequences to their 'own fault' ("I should have been more careful.").

Passages

What stages have you gone through in your financial life?

In traditional marriages of providers and nurturers, I've noticed that very often there's a midlife switch.

Men, having left for the office every day for decades, often suddenly want to be a part of home life. They take a new interest in their children, want to learn Julia Child's secret for French sauces, or decide to build that new addition to the house themselves.

Women, up to their aprons in Julia Child's culinary advice, may want to take a stab at the stock portfolio instead of the chicken cordon bleu. They begin to take ledgers in hand, read Forbes* rather than Fashion, and sit riveted to "Wall Street Week" on television.

Just as you wouldn't want to make a habit of betting on horse races without perusing the racing form and looking over the ponies, you shouldn't enter financial entanglements with your mate without understanding the fundamental differences between you. That means each of you must learn how to interpret the other's codes and to speak the same love/money language.

Male/Female Communication: Love Means Never Having to Say "What Do You Mean?"

"What happened to that last girlfriend you had?" a young stockbroker asked his colleague in the movie *Wall Street*.

"Gone," replied his friend. "She asked the wrong question."

"What question was that?"

"She asked, 'What are you thinking?'"

Men and women don't speak the same language. They may use the same syntax and the same words, but the meanings they attach to those words are profoundly different.

Communication about money is similar to behavior around money—both are learned at a very early age.

Girls are encouraged to communicate verbally. They share secrets, confidences and feelings.

Boys relate by doing things together, in the form of sports and play. Verbal communication is based on recounting of facts (who did what, where, and why).

Women want their men to express themselves in words, to be a new and improved version of their best friend. Men want their actions to speak for them.

When the two sit down at the dinner table and a money conversation looms, she usually wants to talk about it; he'd rather not discuss it—handle it tomorrow and be done with it altogether.

---

* Forbes - a monthly finance magazine.

If the conversation is inevitable, it will be approached from two divergent points of view. Women think talking is a sign that things are going well; men see talks as confrontations, a sure sign things are going wrong.

Men tend to communicate through: *Jokes* ("Uh-oh, another money talk... Better tape my ankles and get out the ol' helmet and shoulder pads..."); *Interpretations* ("I'm sure the bank manager didn't mean that... What he probably meant was..."); and *Advice* ("Here's what you should do...")

Women tend to communicate through: *Confidences* ("I just have to let you know how much this is bothering me"); *Emotional expression* ("My God! Not another bounced check! I'm sure they're going to cancel our account!"); or *Confrontation* ("I want you to do something about this right now.").

When upset, men tend to express themselves through anger; women, through tears. It's easy to see how much valuable communication gets lost in the cross-gender translation:

When men	*Women interpret it as*
Joke	Not caring about her or the problem.
Reinterpret circumstances	Not trusting her point of view.
Advise	Patronizing her, belittling her opinion.

When women	*Men interpret it as*
Confide	Burdening him with unnecessary information.
Express emotions	Making a mountain out of a molehill.
Confront	Henpecking, nagging.

To make matters more complicated, sometimes you're not even talking to your mate as an individual but as a representative of his or her sex. Instead, a man often reacts to the 'female,' rather than to the woman who is his wife. Women react to their partner's maleness. Says a thirty-year old female writer, "Once in a while I'd suggest some business move to my husband—and he'd ignore it or, worse, belittle me. The next day a man could say the very same thing and he'd think it was a brilliant idea. Simply because I'm a woman, my ideas were dismissed." Men, of course, voice similar complaints. "It seems like sometimes my wife blames me for every bad thing men have done in her life," says a 45-year-old chef. "Even though I've never given her any reason to distrust me with money, there are times when she's totally irrational and distrusts me for no other reason than being a man."

Re-examining Your Beliefs About Sex and Money

Both men and women carry around obsolete and utterly dysfunctional beliefs about gender and money. Often those beliefs don't bear up under the scrutiny of hard financial logic. And when used to make your partner appear wrong or stereotyped, they can cut off your relationship at the roots.

Yet, these Hidden Investments of belief in how men and women "are" can be so ingrained and unconscious that they've never been thought about, much less discussed. To see what sex-based Hidden Investments you've accumulated over the years, take the following self-test. Ask your partner to do the same.

1. When I hear the words 'men' and 'money' together, I think (Choose relevant answers):

competent	trouble	accusing	nurturer
desirable	organized	disorganized	spendthrift
experienced	powerful	harebrained	scheming
intuitive	savvy	incompetent	miserly
fair	generous	risky	hoarding
provider	sexy	prudent	wimp

2. When I hear the words 'women' and 'money' together, I think (Choose relevant answers from the list above):

3. In regard to money I believe

   a. a man should _____.
   b. a woman should _____.

4. When

    a. a man talks to me about money I feel _____.
    b. a woman talks to me about money I feel _____.

5. I would trust a man/woman with my money when

    _____.

6. I would never trust a man/woman with my money when

    _____.

Look over your answers and discuss them. If you're like most of my clients who take this test you've probably discovered some very noble attitudes about the opposite sex (and your own sex) you didn't know you had. You also probably found some biases you're not proud of.

Of those Hidden Investments in sexual roles, which ones are current, applying specifically to your own spouse? Which are more appropriately associated with an event and person in your past? Which attitudes serve and support your present relationship? Which ones are you able to change?

The Sexual Politics of Inclusion

Can the war between the sexes be ended, at least as it is fought on the battleground of finance? For Cecilia and Roy, like most couples, the terms of truce are complicated. How do we structure provider and nurturer roles so that each spouse can live a whole, diverse, and fulfilling life? How can we balance the differences between the sexes to include all aspects of human nature?

For years I've seen men come for financial planning, seemingly exhausted from shouldering alone the financial burden of the family. As more and more professions open up to both sexes, the time is passing when men feel forced to sacrifice health and happiness to pay the bills.

As women explore endeavors beyond tending houses and minding children, they are building confidence in making and managing resources at home and in the marketplace.

I offered to Roy and Cecilia, as I'm offering to you, a new way to look at love/money relationships. It demands that we step outside the confines and stereotypes of gender, to appreciate qualities of 'maleness' and 'femaleness' existing in each individual.

For me the ideas of the psychologist Carl Jung were very helpful. According to Jung we all possess various masculine and feminine traits, regardless of our anatomy. How we balance those qualities—and what we do with them—is what determines our destiny.

Those qualities include:

Masculine Attributes	Feminine Attributes
Ordered	Intuitive
Structured	Cyclical
Finite	Connected
Objective	Subjective

Ideally, these two sets of contradictory impulses work together within each person, and in each relationship. The fully integrated love/money marriage can be achieved only through balancing complementary aspects, where masculine and feminine attributes work together harmoniously, with neither one overriding the other.

With Cecilia and Roy, as they began to look closer at the idea of complementary traits, the gravity pulling them into rigid provider and nurturer roles was less compelling. They began to make compromises and find solutions other than those handed down by past generations as "the only way family life can work."

The turning point came when I asked Roy, "Do you realize Cecilia was making and managing money before the baby came? Right here you have someone with the interest and capability to contribute toward your mutual goals."

"I see it," Roy answered, "but it's hard to get past that macho part of me that wants to be 'man enough' to take care of everything."

"Don't you think it's worth it?" I countered. "Look at what it's costing you. You're risking bankruptcy. How far will you go to prove your manliness?"

"Yeah," he finally realized and admitted. "I guess you're right. I'll talk it over with Cecilia. Maybe there is a way she can bring in some extra income without sacrificing her time with Melinda."

Roy and Cecilia eventually worked out a new arrangement. When Cecilia wasn't working, she would preserve all her prior say-so in financial decisions. After a year she did go back to acting, but only after Roy agreed to take on a share of the family's nurturing tasks.

The battle of the sexes has no place between the balance sheets. In today's economy, it's no longer possible for one sex to be the guardian of all financial knowledge while the other keeps love and home fires burning. We should all be equally conversant in the language of money.

Think of areas in which you and your spouse keep the battle going in the financial domain. What Hidden Investments in sexual roles are keeping the conflict armed and dangerous? What skills could be improved, and what aspects of your thinking might be changed to create a more inclusive love/money dynamic?

Chapter THREE

Power Plays, Payback and Other Bad Investments

*Truth #3: When financial power is
hoarded, put-downs lead to paybacks.*

"I can't imagine why he's this late," Lina said, fingering her gold Cartier watch. "He's known about this appointment for weeks. If he worms out of this one I'm going to slap him with a divorce suit that will have him seeing double."

It was Lina and Perry's first financial-planning appointment together. I had been working with Lina for several months on her chaotic personal portfolio. She had brought more than half a million dollars into her marriage, all of which was now committed to Perry's many limited partnership* ventures. The relationship had been rocky from the first, and Lina was nervous.

---

* Limited Partnership – an investment which cannot be easily valued, traded, sold, or converted to cash.

To Lina, it was time to bring Perry in and talk to him frankly about those investments, and Perry was half an hour late. When he finally arrived, I realized immediately what Lina found both attractive and dangerous about him. The man wore his middle age well—tanned, handsome, and drop-dead charming. He lit a cigarette, leaned forward in his chair and broke into a magnanimous smile.

"Well, what's the program here?" he began. "Lina has been bugging me about coming here for months. Now what can I do for you ladies?"

I answered matter-of-factly. "Lina is concerned about the liquidity of the investments you've made in her behalf."

Before I could finish my sentence, Perry launched into a ten-minute speech about how those investments were indeed liquid, how wise and well managed they were, how Lina's best interests were his only concern.

He crafted sentences artfully. Facts were reshaped; financial terms were sprinkled about to lend credibility; hard figures were glossed over quickly. By the end of it, even the most knowledgeable might have been buffaloed into believing those deals really were liquid.

"The definition of liquidity is straightforward," I interjected finally. "Can Lina's assets be converted into cash in one week?"

"If you put it that way—no," he said, his manner darkening.

"Well then, we have some work to do to address Lina's concerns about liquidity and loss of control . . . and to find the optimum diversification mix for your investments," I said.

The Power Paradox

As Lina and Perry were to find out, power is our most coveted commodity. Now more than ever, the currency of power is money. Cold cash can buy a lot of leverage in even the most enlightened and open relationships.

"Power is the ultimate aphrodisiac," a famous politician, known for his success with the world's most desirable women, once said.

Power sustains more romantic interest, in the long run, than Nautilus sculpted physiques and chiseled good looks. You feel power the instant you enter its presence. It's stimulating, magnetic, intriguing, and sexy. Power—or sense of control—is at the heart of every person's self-esteem. It determines how valuable one feels.

Financial power can be wholly positive in an intimate relationship, as well-used wealth kindles passions and commands admiration and respect. When power roles grow rigid, with one partner commanding more clout at the other's expense, relationships go haywire. Spouses begin to see an adversary in the person lying next to them in bed.

Healthy competition is good for a relationship. A rousing game of tennis or an intellectual jousting match boosts self-confidence and releases stress.

But couples who turn every encounter into a win-or-lose proposition are locked in a divisive and dangerous game, in which the partnership stands at stake. Lina and Perry lived in the heat of that game.

According to Lina, Perry had trouble accepting the wealth she had made on her own before they met. "It always aggravated him, as though he were less of a man because of it," she commented more than once.

To remedy what he saw as his diminished importance, Perry set about investing her assets, all with the promise of earning a higher rate of return. In the beginning Lina saw it as a wonderful opportunity—someone she loved and trusted would help her increase her net worth.

As years went by, misgivings festered into full-blown paranoia. Perry no longer consulted her when money was moved around. Lina began to doubt the investments were sound. She hadn't bothered to look at financial statements because she trusted Perry, but when she finally asked for them he offered vague or convoluted explanations.

She began threatening divorce. "I may stay with him and I may not," she once confided. "I want my money where I can get to it if I need it. I came into this marriage with a lot of leverage. I want that leverage back. I'm not going to play the subservient wife."

If the marriage was going to survive, I told Lina, there would have to be some important shifts, and not just shifts of money from his control to hers. There would have to be shifts in perceptions and balances of power.

Power, and how it will be shared, is the most important issue you will face as a couple. To be in a mutually enriching relationship is to tackle that issue head-on every day, and emerge in the end as partners.

Before that can be done in a fully informed manner, it's crucial to understand the ways in which power is abused. Like Lina and Perry, we all abuse it to some degree, in the form of power plays.

Power plays are what you resort to when you don't believe you have real power. When you doubt your own abilities or your partner's intentions, you resort to underhanded tactics and manipulation. True power expresses itself honestly and openly; power plays are just the opposite.

To understand them is to discover why you sometimes feel helpless, manipulated, and weak—and you don't know why. In some cases you'll recognize yourself among the power players I characterize in the pages that follow. You shouldn't blame yourself. Instead, look at which Hidden Investments or fears underlie the power games you play.

Remember, these plays are rarely as clear-cut or as malicious as they may seem. They are somewhat exaggerated here so that you can see these behavior patterns more clearly.

Infantilizers

"Don't worry your pretty little head about it," an infantilizer I knew used to say to his wife. When she would ask about the family finances, his answer was always the same: "You wouldn't understand."

Infantilizers, often men, draw power energy from the father role. "Don't worry, I'll take care of you" is another way of saying "you're incapable of caring for yourself."

Unsure of their own abilities, infantilizers cope by reducing their mate's intelligence and authority. Encouraging their spouses to be financial children, they are then free to have their victories—and make their mistakes—without an intelligent witness.

Women have come to me after years, sometimes decades, of marriage with literally no idea of their financial worth. Usually, after a divorce or the death of the husband, they are left managing a financial life for which they are totally unprepared. "I had no idea we were in this much trouble," one wife said to me, in tears, as it dawned on her that the nest egg her husband had always claimed to be building had never really existed. Assets to oversee—and debts to pay—come as complete surprises. These financial 'infants' are then left with the unenviable task of learning about complex money issues—and solving messes—from scratch, or else finding another parent figure in an accountant, lawyer, or friend to do it for them.

Information Controllers

"What do you mean, we owe ten thousand dollars in back taxes? I didn't even know her store was turning a profit," a shocked husband once complained to me, upon finding out his wife had been concealing money she had earned in her business.

Knowledge is power. Information controllers know it. No one else in their lives knows the whole truth about their finances. Like poker players, they use pieces of information like playing cards. They pick up a few here, show a few there, never letting anyone see their hand until they're ready. Even then, there is usually a card hidden up a sleeve.

They lie about profits and losses. They're ambiguous and evasive when questioned. They conceal documents that might give them away. When pressed for facts they lash out, "I don't want to talk about it!"

These power players dole out information piecemeal, in small, insubstantial quantities. They keep intimates powerless by controlling what they know or don't know. Under the guise of being tactful ("He/she doesn't really want/need to know all that"), they re-create financial reality to fit the way they want it to look.

Furthermore, typically, they want to know everything about everyone else. They ask questions and probe for answers. The more they know about others—and the less others know about them—the more powerful they feel. Spouses are susceptible to this power play when their own sense of reality isn't sharply defined. Ignorant of their own bottom line, they don't know when—or how—to call the information controller's bluff.

Money Martyrs

"All I do for you, and this is the thanks I get," is the money martyr's typical complaint. What they don't mention is that no one can ever thank them enough.

"I feel so guilty spending money," their spouses often say. Guilt, of course, is what keeps money martyrs in business. Their lovers and spouses are so busy feeling undeserving, they don't take time to consider their own wants and needs. They rarely ask, "What do I deserve?"

Money martyrs come disguised as nurturers with a seemingly endless capacity to give. Their gifts, however, aren't ever free. You might recognize one of these power players:

- The wife who says she can't possibly buy a new dress because the kids need designer jeans.

- The husband who never fails to mention that he clocks in every day, at a job he hates, so that his family can live in comfort and his wife doesn't have to work.

Money martyrs suffer. And they suffer grandly. All the world knows how hard they toil under the thumb of adversity, and that their lot in life is so very unrewarding. Appearing to sacrifice everything, they play a spouse's guilt like a violin, knowing which string to pluck to get the desired response.

Loved ones knock themselves out to serve these power players, trying to settle a debt they don't remember incurring—and that 'debt' is never paid off.

Unilateral Decision Makers

"What the hell do you mean you went out and bought a car? Did it ever occur to you I might have something to say about it?" an irate wife screamed at her husband.

To her, his one-way decision to drive home a new Toyota showed blatant disregard for her feelings and their mutual goals. To him, the unilateral decision was an exercise in his right to "do what I damn well please with my own money, thank you."

Unilateral decision makers aren't always tyrants. They're power players who feel their power through spending money, without having to kow-tow to anyone else. They feel their independence only when free of the needs and opinions of others.

They're ingenious in the many ways they can save and spend money without their partners knowing it:

- They buy themselves a new stereo with rent money.

- They take out loans without anyone's knowledge.

- Purchases—clothes, shoes, skis, toasters, jewelry—magically appear around the house.

- Funds disappear just as magically.

Intimates of these power players feel neglected and left out. Their opinions are overruled and their feelings ignored.

Money Rebels

"I'll do it when I want to . . . if I want to," the money rebel says when asked to meet any financial obligation: pay taxes, send the rent payment, record checks.

Rebels feel they've been forced into a financial world they never asked to be a part of. Every financial responsibility represents an unwelcome intrusion into an otherwise wonderful day. They ab- hor demands ad outside authority. The demands of earning and managing money constitute the consummate outside authority.

They rebel by:

- *Evading:* A young rebel I knew took elaborate steps to avoid taxes, even entering into illegal schemes in order to keep her financial resources "outside the system."

- *Sabotaging:* The husband of one of my clients 'lost' the enve- lopes containing the family's tax returns and checks made out to the I.R.S. The fact that the taxes hadn't been paid wasn't discovered by his wife until months later.

Many of us have a bit of the money rebel in us. The power play is there when we don't write down checks, when we go out to a res- taurant we can't afford, when we fudge on taxes.

Damage is done to relationships when rebellion against the demands of the financial world and society is projected onto a hapless mate. When the rebel's spouse suddenly becomes the enemy, all mutual goals and duties become a target of rebellion. Intimates are cast as obsessive nit-pickers—parent substitutes to be avoided or, preferably, overpowered.

Benevolent Manipulators

"You're making a mountain out of a molehill," benevolent manipulators say when you throw a fit because their business has never made it out of the red. They soothe, mollify and disarm you: "Now, have I ever let you down?"

Benevolent manipulators soften the hard edges of truth by making their spouses feel that problems are the products of an overactive imagination. Their commands are coated with sugar; their edicts are kindhearted monologues full of words like 'honey' and 'dear.'

A male friend of mine was married to just such a benevolent manipulator. "How do you feel about this?" she would ask him. Then, when he offered up real feelings, she would appear shocked, as "I can't believe you feel that way."

Under the cover of kindness, they reshape truth. Using words as smokescreens, benevolent manipulators get their way by tailor-making reality to their own specifications.

Police have been known to play "good cop/bad cop" as a psychological strategy for interrogating suspects. The 'bad cop' screams, threatens, and accuses the suspect, making the 'good cop' appear a trusted friend to be confided in.

Benevolent manipulators are the perennial 'good cop.' They extract information and fulfill their wishes in a tactical game so impeccable and seamlesss their spouses are left feeling silly and thankful that they finally see the light.

Benevolent manipulators dominate by:

- *Cajoling*: "Now you know how bad you are with numbers, don't you?"

- *Coaxing*: "Oh, come on, you balance those accounts. You're so much better at it than I am."

- *Needling*: "How many times have I told you not to send extra money to your ex-wife? She doesn't need it as much as we do, now does she?"
- *Promises*: "When we can afford it, I promise you'll get everything you want. Just trust me and sacrifice a little right now."

Benevolent manipulators honor the form of honest collaboration, but abuse the essence. Appearing to communicate openly, they use words to create confusion. Appearing to share power with their partners, they entice intimates into surrendering all power to them.

Helpless Manipulators

"I'm just no good with money. You'll handle all that stuff for me, won't you, honey?" Who, you might ask, would choose ignorance over intelligence?

More people than you would imagine. The ranks of the 'financially helpless' are divided into two categories:

- Those who can't—lack sufficient education or mental acuity to comprehend basic financial concepts; or, individuals whose impulses are so out of control they are helpless to direct the inflow and outflow of financial resources.
- Those who won't—make a point of never learning financial concepts and practices; adults who consciously choose to remain financial children and refine helplessness to an art.

The latter group are formidable power players. "Please take care of me" is the hook they use to reel in their mates. Attracting spouses who want to be heroes, the helpless manipulators become powerful by concealing their true power.

Feigning helplessness is one of the most devious power plays. Those who *can't* take financial responsibility for themselves are indistinguishable from those who simply *won't*.

Women have been well schooled in 'learned helplessness.' The character Blanche DuBois in *A Streetcar Named Desire* speaks the ode of 'helpless' women everywhere when she says in her sweetest Southern lilt, "I have always depended upon the kindness of strangers."

Though men have developed their own tactics for using helplessness, women still have more permission for acting vulnerable.

In some circles vulnerability is still considered quintessentially feminine.

Money Saviors

"Thank God I came along in your life," saviors say to their mates. Like money martyrs, saviors disguise acts of dominance as gestures of generosity. Instead of using guilt to manipulate, they use their partner's own self-doubt to gain power. They portray the acquisition and management of money as an arcane skill only they have mastered.

A forty-year-old saleswoman, whose husband was never able to hold down a job, used to say, "I don't know what he would have done without me—look through other people's trash for recyclable beer cans, probably."

Money saviors choose partners who are vulnerable to them: men and women in precarious financial circumstances who are uncertain of their own talents. Saviors never support their partners in learning to save themselves. They're stronger knowing they've saved the one they love from certain financial ruin.

Learning financial lessons isn't always fun. And profound insights often come painfully. Financial losses help you distinguish good deals from bad deals in the future. Running out of money can make you more diligent in budgeting the next month. By supporting and amplifying their partners' inherent weaknesses, saviors simply keep the crippled partner at bay. Like the spouse of an alcoholic who says, "A little wine with dinner won't hurt you," saviors kill with kindness.

Power Intimidators

"Just remember, you can be out on the street in no time," power intimidators say, or imply, whenever their authority is questioned. They pack their ammunition in their wallets. They can bestow or take away financial security, and they use that position at every turn.

"Do as I say—or else," is the ultimatum that ends all debate.

These players see their mate's opinions as obstacles to overcome—by force if necessary. They scream, swear, threaten, belittle, and needle. They manipulate with their anger. Getting mad means getting their way, and that anger has a hair trigger, always ready to go off.

Spouses respond by playing peacemaker. They placate and soothe the intimidator, giving in yet again to avoid trouble and anything this spouse says or does can suddenly become trouble. Rather than taking steps to muster their own power, the spouses watch their words and follow orders, sinking deeper into financial dependency.

The overtly tyrannical are also the most overtly violent. It is often with this type of power player that money conflicts result in physical or psychological abuse.

Spotting the 'Bad Players' In Your Life

Most garden-variety power plays you encounter or participate in are innocent enough. They are a normal way of getting back on top after a perceived slip in self-esteem. In most relationships they're balanced by other more open, loving forms of interaction. Nevertheless, lest we be Pollyanna's about this, it's important to talk about power plays that are not harmless at all.

A client of mine once came home from work to find all her furniture in a moving van. Her husband was standing in the front yard watching the remainder of the bedroom set being loaded.

"What's going on?" she demanded, suddenly sickened by the memory that only the week before, he'd coerced her into signing over all their joint assets to him ('Tax savings,' she'd reasoned).

"We're getting a divorce. I want out. My lawyers will be calling you."

We'd all like to think those we love and trust would never hurt us. Truth is, sometimes they deliberately do. At first it may be difficult to spot the con man lurking beneath the charming smile, the gold digger behind the innocent eyes. Love can lead even skeptics into relationships with compulsive liars or cheats.

It would be nice if every love/money relationship could be salvaged. The fact is, there are some people who simply do not respond to financial or psychological counseling, people who won't listen and won't change.

If you are involved with such a 'bad player,' you will have to ask yourself some hard questions, and perhaps face facts you'd rather ignore. Is the relationship you're in worth what it's costing you? Are you having to act dishonestly? Are you frightened of creditors or others because of your partner's behavior? Do you feel trapped financially and emotionally?

Only you can determine what's best for your life—but just as you should not tolerate physical abuse, you should also not submit to financial tyranny.

Put-downs Always Lead to Paybacks

How can anyone stand there and passively take all that abuse from power players? The truth is that most don't. From what I've seen, put-downs always lead to paybacks. A payback is a sting—an overt or camouflaged retaliation for a partner's behavior. It conveys everything from frustration to fury, without the need to exchange one word.

Paybacks take many forms, as obvious as an extravagant purchase or as subtle as a bounced check. They can be directly related to an offense (she splurges on new luggage; he buys a new VCR) or apparently unrelated (he drops a lot of money on a bad stock tip; she refuses to take their traditional vacation to the lake).

Paybacks are one-two punches delivering both hidden and direct messages. The tactic is so effective and dangerous precisely because it's camouflaged. Almost invisible beneath the veneer of normalcy, the attack frustrates and confuses the victim, because an act of aggression appears as an innocent act of forgetfulness or an 'act of God.'

The payback plays upon expectations. The greater the expectation and the more intimate the relationship, the more painful the payback. In the long run, however, it usually hurts the perpetrator as much as the victim, encouraging the very behavior it meant to punish. I am sure you'll recognize the more common paybacks:

Revenge Spending

A woman retaliated for her husband's spending money on his children and ex-wife with what I called "plastic revenge." Whenever he would send the prior family gifts or money, she would hit the department stores and, with no agreement from him, make sure she was well compensated. Revenge spending is tit for tat, plain and simple. He deprives her of control by committing money to his children. She runs up their debts—and debt service.

Skimming

The practice of skimming is practically ritualized among relationships in which one partner wields total control over the household wealth. In the early stages, skimmers innocently overestimate the cost of grocery expenses or school clothes for the kids. I've seen it progress to premeditated theft: secreting money out of billfolds and altering checkbooks.

When partners don't experience their earning power or the ability to possess resources, they usually discover roundabout ways to circumvent the power structure. Skimming is a way of feeling a modicum of self-determination.

Sexual Revenge

Money and sex. Both can bond couples into physical and spiritual partnerships. Both are also power tools, wedges partners use to gain leverage over each other.

Some pay back by withholding sex. Others pay back by having sex, in the form of extramarital liaisons. I've seen too many affairs occur in relationships where money and power conflicts are present. Look a little deeper at those cases and you'll usually find more than simple lack of sexual interest in a spouse or uncontrollable passion for a prospective lover. Partners deprived of financial power tend to compensate by using, and abusing, the powers they do have. The power to have and refuse sex is granted to all of us equally.

Looking at Your Own Power Use (and Abuse)

To get to the control center of the power problem is to know what money and power represent to you and your partner. What

Hidden Investments in power are you carrying in your psychological portfolio?

Take a moment to ask yourself the following:

1. What is my definition of power?

2. How powerful did I feel in my family?

3. Was power balanced in previous love/money relationships?

4. What does surrendering power to my partner mean to me?

5. What 'powers' do I believe money buys me in my present relationship?

6. In what way do I wield power over my partner and get him/her to do what I want?

7. How much am I compensating for past feelings of powerlessness?

Discuss your answers with your partner. Are there aspects of power you find desirable and supportive? Are there power plays you're using that are divisive and destructive? How are those Hidden Investments in power showing up in your financial portfolio?

Often, the behaviors we imagine bring us power only conceal and exaggerate a deeper sense of weakness.

Realizing their marriage was about to contribute to the rise in money-related divorce statistics, Lina and Perry spent an entire weekend with this exercise. When they came back to my office, much had changed.

"I didn't know Perry had such a hard time with money in his early life. He suffered a lot," said Lina. "He craves power now because he had so little of it early on."

"Yes, and Lina isn't another one of the many who are out to get me," joked Perry. "I'm learning to see her not as the enemy."

Whenever there's a power struggle in your psychological portfolio, it shows up, down the line, in the financial portfolio. The two are always related.

Maybe your finances are in good shape, but trouble smolders in your sex life. Or conversely, maybe you can keep your power struggles hidden from your friends, but your monetary success keeps getting sabotaged.

"How can I get Perry to change, to include me more, to be more accepting of my wealth and abilities?" Lina asked me, when it came time to change those power dynamics in her marriage. "His ways have been serving him for a long time."

It's true. He or she who holds the power rarely yields it without a struggle. Nevertheless, surprising changes can take place when controlling spouses such as Perry see that it is in their best interests to share the wealth.

Cost/Benefit Analysis

Cost/benefit analysis is a prerequisite to all business transactions: *What will you get versus what it will cost.* Why should the business of relationships be any different? As we're seeing, power imbalances are emotionally destructive and financially unprofitable. The cost/benefit analysis looks like this:

Power Imbalanced

Situation:

Perry made a unilateral decision and invested in a new shopping center.

Cost:

Lina is irate. She grows suspicious, cold, and unloving. She builds a case that Perry is trying to take her money. She threatens divorce. Perry feels frustrated and unfairly accused. The money is suddenly at stake as talk of litigation grows more serious.

Benefit (real or perceived):

Perry gets to make the deal he wants to make, using Lina's assets without having to answer to her opinions. Lina doesn't have to take responsibility for the investment. If it's a wise one, she profits. If not, she blames Perry.

Clearly, in this case, the costs outweigh the benefits. Perry may have satisfied a short run need, but he can count on a counter power move, in some form, in the future. And that move might even be divorce.

Situation:

Perry thinks a new shopping center is a great investment and Lina has some liquid assets. He shows her the deal and asks her what she thinks. She agrees. The opportunity looks good.

Cost:

Perry had to take the time to consult Lina and run the risk that she might say no. Lina had to take on the risk involved in the decision, rather than heaping the responsibility onto Perry's shoulders.

Benefit (real or perceived):

They both are in on a good investment deal and money is well used. They build trust and cooperation which will serve them well in reaching mutual goals.

Think about a financial situation currently interfering with the power balance in your relationship. Consider the costs and benefits as Lina and Perry did. Consider and discuss compromise solutions that could reduce the costs and raise the benefits.

Mapping Your Turf

There are certain domains in your life you may consider sacrosanct. Your partner has no right to interfere without permission. While an open-door policy is a terrific ideal in marriages, many individuals arrive at a point where they feel invaded, identity lost and power usurped.

A good way to preserve your sense of self-determination—and neutralize a partner's power plays—is to map out your personal financial turf.

What are the decisions you absolutely must make on your own or be included in when your spouse makes them? Under what circumstances is it all right to defer?

Lina mapped her turf this way:

I need to...

- be an equal partner in all decisions concerning the $500,000 I brought into this relationship and all our community property.
- be respected and appreciated for the financial knowledge I have.
- have a certain sum of that money—$80,000—liquid for my private use.

It's all right if...

- Perry makes unilateral decisions regarding his personal money.
- Perry manages the financial details like banking, budgeting, and paperwork—details I hate. I will defer to him on those matters.

Having your turf respected also means respecting your partner's power needs. Tune in to his/her sources of self-esteem power, and respect them. Mapping out your relationship turf means knowing where both treasures and dangers lie.

When financial power is hoarded, put-downs always lead to paybacks. When power moves like an electrical current, freely through a relationship, it becomes a formidable and energizing force. In fact, it gathers and gives off more wattage than either individual partner could muster on his or her own. We are always more powerful, financially and romantically, when we act together. Think of the power plays in which you recognized parts of yourself or your partner. In the past few months, have there been some paybacks exchanged between you? Are there some areas in your power dynamics that could use some rebalancing and change?

Chapter FOUR

Miscommunication, Misunderstandings and Moneyspeak

Truth #4: The better you manage your money talk, the better you'll manage your money.

"**I**'ve learned to dread those little heart-to-heart talks about money," said Aaron. "We start out fine, but things have a way of snowballing. Usually we end up in a rip-roaring fight—even when the topic was whether or not we should buy a new lawn mower. Money's a subject we go out of our way to avoid.

"First we tiptoe around the subject, going real slow and being real nice. Then one of us will say something that sounds like an attack on the other—and watch out. We're in a knockdown drag-out fight in no time. And once that gets going, there's no stopping until one or both of us gets hurt. "

Aaron and Camille came to me with a common problem. They knew how to make money—and how to spend it. They just couldn't talk about it.

They aren't alone. Most couples, at some point, fight about money. At their best, such tiffs are a way of clearing the air and blowing off steam. Cyclical and recurring money fights, however, in which couples go round after round with each other and get nothing resolved, can be catastrophic.

Talking about the volatile subject of money is an art and science I call 'moneyspeak.' Some do it well, simply by knowing intuitively how to phrase concerns and respond to anger. Others break down very early in the exchange.

Do you find yourself in a confront-and-defend syndrome? Do you keep hitting the same 'hot spots'—topics of debate that, like a poison ivy rash, disappear for a while, then pop up somewhere else? Or do you avoid overt discussion, and communicate in more covert ways?

When daily financial issues arise, you will moneyspeak in one of three ways: by *colliding, colluding,* or *collaborating.*

We'll take a long look at these three dynamics. First, it will help to look at the way society shapes our moneyspeak. Why does everyone find money so darned hard to talk about?

The Money Taboo

"What do you owe?" "How much do you make?" "Who makes more, you or your spouse?"

These are not the typical conversation starters of polite society. We consider such intrusions personal, embarrassing, and outright rude.

In this tell-all, expose-all culture, bedroom adventures have to be extraordinary even to rate as good gossip. Discussing the terms of a prenuptial contract, however, or even how much one's house cost, is quite another matter.

The paradox shows up every time we meet another person and begin to talk money. We are a society obsessed by economics. The subject of the stock market or the latest corporate takeover is preferred cocktail-party dish while, on the other hand, conversations about the more personal aspects of money are regulated by more rules of etiquette than a Japanese tea ceremony.

While the subject of macro-economics is bandied about without restriction, issues of micro-economics are taken into private quarters and whispered about.

Once a little girl came up to me and, noticing the diamond on my wedding ring, guilelessly blurted, "Wow, that's pretty! You must be rich!" Her mother, standing nearby, was mortified.

In these liberal times, why is the subject of one's money so touchy? If wealth is something to be proud of, why is it embarrassing to openly, verbally claim it?

The money taboo goes back to antiquity. The sensitivity of the subject has its origins as a pragmatic axiom: Don't tell people how much you have because they will steal it.

Down through the centuries, money taboos have grown more intricate. As Ralph Waldo Emerson observed in 1844, "Money . . . is hardly spoken of in parlors without an apology."

Money today—more than ever—has been identified with the deepest forms of self-esteem and self-worth. As a society we have a Hidden Investment in financial value as a gauge of personal value. Income doesn't simply mean 'what I earn.' For many, it's synonymous with 'who I am.' It's a statement of identity of the most intimate sort.

The correlation between money and self-esteem can have tragic results. We've all heard stories of men who are fired at work and yet get dressed every morning and leave the house as usual. They never tell their families about losing their jobs until they've found a new one to replace it. People have been known to commit crimes, even suicide, rather than admit financial failure.

The taboo doesn't disappear when we fall in love or get married. In some ways, it just gets more complicated. Everyone wants to be deemed worthy in the eyes of a lover. If money makes you more worthy, then talking frankly about it is a vulnerable, self-revealing gesture.

According to sociologists Blumstein and Schwartz (*American Couples*), couples are more comfortable divulging to each other the details of their prior sex lives than they are sharing the intimacies of finance. Each relationship develops its own quirky ways of navigating around the topic.

Sometimes money issues show up in disguise. What is, at heart, a money fight can masquerade as a blowup over who will wash the car or which relative to have Thanksgiving dinner with. In the middle of a slugfest over some trivial problem, few couples stop long enough to ask themselves, "Is it money we're really fighting about, or is it something else?"

Among couples where the subject is more easily broached, the masquerade is often reversed: Money fights substitute for confrontations over deeper problems. One client couple I met with, for example, discovered in therapy that sexual issues were the real source of the tension between them. For years, bedroom life was rarely mentioned, but they were quick to collide over credit card bills and how much to tip the babysitter.

Money today is too important an issue to remain confused about. It's time to put those taboos into perspective, to reevaluate net worth as a barometer for self-esteem. It's time to talk about money openly, in terms of what it really is: a matter of dollars and cents.

To do that requires *moneyspeak* mastery. If money talk goes on easily in your home, you intuitively understand how to collaborate. If there are tensions and resentments, however, chances are good you're either colliding or colluding.

Collisions and Free-For-All's

Aaron and Camille described to me in detail their last money fight. The catalyst, for them, was a common one. A check overdraft slip showed up in the mail.

AARON: *Damn it! We bounced another check. How could this happen? Didn't you balance the checkbook?*

CAMILLE: *And why is it always my responsibility to balance the checkbook?*

AARON: *Because I work all day long. You know your work hours are more flexible.*

CAMILLE: *Even with both our salaries we can't keep enough money in the bank because you pay all that alimony to your ex-wife.*

AARON: *At least she doesn't waste it all on clothes. Every spare nickel we make goes into your wardrobe.*

CAMILLE: *Fortunately, shopping gives me something to do on weekends. You spend all your free time on the golf course.*

The typical money fight is a *collision*—two parties, each with accelerating anger and an unyielding point of view, set a course for direct confrontation.

Once engaged, the fight cycle is self-perpetuating. Pent-up emotions and withheld anger from past incidents are blurted out at the very time when it's nearly impossible to communicate productively. Both spouses begin jockeying for position, using any power plays they know, to maneuver their way back on top.

There are no rules for controlling irrational behavior and emotions, and rarely any constructive results in indulging them. Typical money fights follow predictable patterns:

The Trigger

It might be a bounced check, a new purchase, an overdue bill. An event or circumstance causes instability. For Aaron and Camille, the trigger was a bounced check.

The First Strike

Either an initial flare-up or steps toward 'working it out.' Couples with the best intentions often launch into explaining their positions, "This is why I'm right. This is why you're wrong." Aaron explains he was counting on Camille to deal with the checkbook.

Symbol Loading

Hidden Investments tend to translate previously neutral words such as 'checkbook' into apparent attacks. Partners no longer hear the words themselves, but translate them (based on past beliefs and experiences) into threats to their competence, self-esteem, freedom, or value.

Explosions on one side set off counterexplosions on the other, and the argument mushrooms. Camille hears Aaron's reprimand as a comment on her personal abilities in general, not check-writing in particular. Aaron receives Camille's barb about his alimony payments as an assault on his position as a provider and husband.

All Systems Go

Most money fights have a quality of inevitability—they're traps waiting to be sprung. Once engaged, the fight cycle becomes automatic, with most of the communication emanating from kneejerk reactions instead of conscious choice.

If the scales of power in the relationship are fairly balanced, the argument will go back and forth: One defends; the other argues. The barrage includes attacks, explanations, counteroffensives, and sharp under-the-table jabs.

His ex-wife, her shopping habits, his golf game—nothing is too sacred or irrelevant. Everything is fair game and can be tossed into the melee.

When there is a great disparity in the power balance, the argument will go underground. The 'weaker' partner will often employ the familiar 'delay and pay back' power play, in which revenge will be exacted, in an apparently unrelated form, in the future.

Peace ... For Now

Collision fights create distance rather than understanding and change. They don't deter the fight the next time the trigger is pulled. And the trigger will inevitably be pulled again.

For Aaron and Camille, this was only one of many such spats over alimony, the use of free time, and earning power. If moneyspeak patterns aren't resolved, those issues will continue to come back.

Collisions usually end with the surrender of one partner, with both giving up in disgust, or with a superficial sense of resolve.

Collusions and Conspiracies of Silence

Unlike above-board money fights, a collusion is a conspiracy—an implicit agreement for wrongful reasons within a relationship that maintains a state of quasi-harmony. Open collisions are rare.

Have you ever met a couple who insisted, "Oh, we never fight about money." Yet you got the feeling that all was not right between them financially?

Colluding couples are everywhere, but they're hard to spot. Unlike colliders who fight in every setting from the bedroom to the supermarket line, the colluders engage in moneyspeak without words.

Not all collusions are evil or nefarious. We all collude to some degree. Most of us have lived successfully with our partners because we know the emotional areas over which to tread lightly. We've learned to adapt to their quirks, to keep their secrets and compensate for their flaws.

For example, one couple who always maintained a tight budget had set ways of 'allowing' each other to overspend. The mere suggestion of going clothes-shopping was a tacit signal that the rules no longer applied. Every other financial matter was open for discussion and scrutiny. The occasional shopping sprees they never talked about.

Some colluders trade money for other things. A wealthy man I knew had a silent agreement with his wife: She could spend as much money as she wanted if she agreed not to get mad about his frequent business trips. He didn't appreciate returning home to enormous bills; nor did she relish the many nights spent alone, but they said nothing to each other. Each was silently paying a price—and silently being reimbursed.

One of the classic money collusions is the spend-scold cycle, immortalized on television's *I Love Lucy*. Countless episodes pivoted on one theme: Lucy would spend money on something, then return home to await Ricky's disapproval. On cue, Ricky inevitably discovered the item and threw a fit. Lucy usually got to keep her purchase, but not without being properly chastised and "learning her lesson." Ricky got to feel the surge of manly authority through his control over both Lucy and the money she spent.

Collusions are also at the heart of all power struggles. Whenever you meet a power player, there will always be a mate who colludes with him or her. Money martyrs and their spouses collude on the basis of guilt. Intimidators collude with their partners on the basis of fear. For every abusive mate there is someone willing to take the blows.

Collusions are like dances. Although one partner may initiate the pattern, it takes two to collude. Conflicts are embedded invisibly. Communication is circuitous, indirect. There is a beguiling illusion of peace, without the open dialogue and power-sharing of collaborative moneyspeak.

In collusions, players have a huge emotional stake in the parts they play. They usually don't see change as an option. Whereas colliders know their fights get them nowhere, colluders believe they're profiting from the game.

We've all seen (or experienced) collusions that are so integral to the foundation of a relationship that we can't imagine the union existing any other way.

One such couple was Dave and Alicia. When they came to me for financial planning, I thought the case would be a cinch—managing the growing assets of two young artists.

Right from the beginning, though, something wasn't right.

"When you had the value of your gallery business estimated, how much did they calculate it to be worth?" I asked Dave matter-of-factly. I expected to hear a simple, dollar-value bottom line.

He stammered and began to tell the story of how difficult it was to calculate. I questioned further. He sidetracked.

The conversation went no more smoothly when I asked them about expenses.

"Our monthly nut is about three grand," offered Dave.

"No, it isn't," insisted Alicia. "We spend almost five thousand dollars."

I looked over their list of expenses. A quick tally added everything up to about $3,000. Was Alicia lying? Why? What was going on with this couple?

After the first few sessions ended with the same inconclusive results, Dave and Alicia began canceling appointments. Soon they quit coming altogether.

Months later I heard the finale of the story from a mutual friend. Alicia had walked out of the marriage, but not without a sizable 'war chest.' She had been siphoning money off the top every month in preparation for financial life on her own. Her plan wasn't altogether lost on Dave, who was undervaluing his business so he'd lose less money when the time came to split the co-mingled property.

Dave and Alicia weren't just lying to me and to each other on this isolated occasion. They had been living together, in pseudo-harmony, with this hidden agenda for years.

Like patients who spend huge sums of money on therapy, then lie to their therapists, colluding couples can be a financial planner's nightmare. When vast areas of financial life are denied or obscured by lies, creating a workable money plan is impossible.

Anatomy of a Collusion

Like collisions, collusions follow specific and predictable stages:

A Difference Surfaces

At some point, Dave and Alicia realized they were no longer in love. Maybe their interests were different. Or their emotional lives diverged.

The Perceived Threat

Both realized divorce was a distinct possibility, and each one's own financial well-being was at stake.

Colluding Behavior Surfaces

Neither one was willing to go above board and voice true feelings. It was not a good time financially to be getting a divorce, they reasoned. Both would end up losers. So each began to contrive and, eventually, lie.

The Payoff

Dave and Alicia postponed the inevitable. He built his business. She feathered her own nest, secretly. They both appeared to be getting what they wanted. The status quo was maintained. Their friends thought they were a perfect couple. Since the truth was never stated by either one, there was never an opportunity to stop the collusion and save the relationship. They kept the pattern going until the day Alicia left.

From Crisis to Collaboration

Of course, most of us collide and collude with our partners to some degree.

Only the most saintly among us never let fly a below-the-belt zinger, never start a screaming match, never stop a partner from making an absolutely awful financial choice because of our own secret motives.

The alternatives, however, are a lot more financially lucrative and emotionally rewarding. They lie in the art of collaborative moneyspeak. Before *collaboration* can even begin, you'll first have to interrupt the colliding and colluding patterns that have become so familiar to you.

Heading Off the Collision and Exposing the Collusion

If you're ever to stop colliding with each other over money, at least one of you has to be willing to resist the temptation to return fire after the first strike. Here are some suggestions I gave to Aaron and Camille which have helped them derail those collisions before they happen:

- ✓ Try the famous 'count to ten' trick: Take a deep breath and count to ten before you answer your partner.

- ✓ Set up a signal, a warning flag that reminds you when you are headed into dangerous territory. It might be the tension visible in your partner's face. Or, trouble follows every time your partner starts a sentence with "Now, look here . . ."

- ✓ When you see the signs of a collision, ask your partner about his or her feelings. Shift the focus away from blaming you and onto acknowledging feelings. That alone could reduce the pressure.

- ✓ When the crash appears inevitable, take a timeout. Walk away. Come back to the problem later, in a different emotional state.

A collusive pattern is not only hard to spot, it's hard to break. Both sides get something out of this conspiracy, so with any attempt to expose it, one side will do everything possible to pull the other back into the game. Here are some suggestions for interrupting a collusive pattern:

- ✓ Tell the truth, period. Collusions are fed by half-truths and omissions.

✓ Keep a list of specific guidelines and agreements, so you don't get lulled into constantly pushing back the line of what's acceptable and what's not. I deal with colluding over-spenders, for example, by having them write down everything they buy for an entire month. When they enter a tempting situation, they carry with them a list of rules, with such agreements as "I will not use credit cards" and "I'll only buy what I really need."

✓ Get a reality check, an outside observer to help you see the dynamics you are sometimes too close to. A financial planner or therapist can point out colluding behavior to help you stop the cycle before it engages.

Collaborative Moneyspeak

Moneyspeak based on collaboration is a creative, dynamic, and disciplined way of communicating about money. It offers a way to navigate those tricky money talks, to communicate anger, apprehension, secrets, and plans without fanning into a five-alarm argument.

To move their communication from insult-hurling contests to a more fruitful form of moneyspeak, I suggested that Camille and Aaron use a new pattern of exchange. I re-created for them a dialogue on the same subject that touched off their previous fight, yet this exchange reflected all the essential elements of collaboration-oriented moneyspeak:

AARON: *Uh-oh. Bad news. We bounced another check. This is the second one this month, and I'm feeling pretty mad about it. What can I do—and what can we do—so this doesn't keep happening?*

CAMILLE: *I wrote that check. God, I feel bad about it. We ran out of money last week and it's been hard keeping any re-serves in the bank accounts. Obviously we need either to spend less or make more. That'll be hard with all our commitments.*

AARON: *Yeah, but if we put our heads together, we can do it. Let's start by making a new budget and cutting back a little. I'll cut back on the golf and save money on the greens fees, if*

*you'll cool it a little down at the mall. In the meantime, I'll
renegotiate some of those commitments. Maybe we can cut
our expenses by doing a little refinancing. Deal?*

CAMILLE: *Deal.*

Like collisions and collusions, collaborations have specific
steps, sequences, and protocols to follow:

The Catalyst

Partners whose power relationship is balanced and open encounter a money issue—job loss, sudden debt, an investment decision. The catalyst came to Aaron and Camille in the form of a
bounced check.

The Fair Fight

Each partner is allowed to vent emotions. Then it's time to sit
down and communicate focally toward a resolution. Focal communicating is the mechanism of productive moneyspeak—and
we'll be looking at how it works much more closely in the following pages.

In the example of collaborative moneyspeak above, Aaron and
Camille illustrated the process magnificently in the way they
avoided blaming each other and focused only on the subject at
hand.

Negotiating a Deal

Instead of the colluders' evade-and-ambush tactics and the
colliders' open warfare, collaborators negotiate toward a settle-
ment. Few money differences are not open to compromise. Aaron
loosened up on his golfing schedule while Camille cut back on her
shopping.

Resolve

When money issues are truly resolved, symbolically loaded
words no longer pack their previous punch. Tensions don't show
up in cyclical arguments or in disabling collusions. Money becomes emotionally neutral, so partners can feel compassion without threat.

Aaron really understood Camille's mistake, and recognized his
own part in the problem of insufficient funds. Camille felt sup-

ported and loved. They went on to solve the overdraft problem in their financial portfolio without emotional interference.

Communication and Collaboration

Once there were ritualized ways for couples to deal with touchy or taboo subjects like money. Often they went through intermediaries, in the form of priests and parents, who would communicate for them—decide upon dowries, mediate differences, and the like.

Just as often, couples would say nothing about their problems, trusting their traditional love/money roles to help them wait out financial storms.

Today, those options won't do. We're in desperate need of new rituals, of well-defined paths we can follow to help us make it through the thicket of modern financial life. Focal communicating is just such a ritual.

When something is the focal point, it's the center of attention. In focal communicating, you are deliberately making a specific money issue the sole center around which your conversation will revolve. This doesn't mean that you turn a talk with your partner into a cold, calculated business conference. Rather, both of you agree to use the skills of focal communicating instead of allowing exchanges to deteriorate into collisions or collusions.

Those skills break down into five main guidelines:

1. Establish a safe place between you.

If you're like most people, you have all the right reasons for initiating money talks; but you tend to do it in all the wrong places at all the wrong times.

Zooming down the freeway is not the best time to confront your husband about his spending habits; when she's rushing out the door is not the optimum moment to ask your wife about an investment. And I've met few people with any love life to speak of who make a habit of talking about money in bed.

The first rule of focal communicating is to establish a physically and emotionally safe place in which to talk to your partner about money.

It may involve a specific location or time of day. Maybe you need to talk money only in the evenings when the kids are in bed and the house has quieted down. Or your safe place might take the form of a brisk walk in the park, away from the distractions of home life.

It may involve a quality of interaction. One couple I knew preferred to hold hands, or touch in some way, while they went over difficult love/money terrain. To them, physical touch was a way of connecting intimately in a discussion that might otherwise have created distance.

A safe place is a highly individual environment, tailor-made to suit your definition of security. It's also a quality of rapport, free of judgment, criticism, and blame. In your safe place, amnesty is granted and a truce declared about all extraneous conflicts. You know you'll be treated—and will treat your partner—with understanding and compassion.

2. Discuss only the subject at hand.

When Aaron and Camille bounced the check, the ensuing discussion was about the overdraft—and everything else they could think to be mad about: shopping, golf, and an ex-wife included.

Money is one of those magnetic topics. It pulls in far-flung and unrelated subjects by sheer force of its emotional power. The only way I know to keep simple discussions from mushrooming into free-for-all's is to discuss *only* the subject at hand.

Moneyspeak within such tight boundaries is like skiing—it looks a lot easier than it is. If you're going to talk about bills, in other words, you absolutely do not talk about earnings. If you're communicating anger about your spouse's overspending, resist the urge to comment on how fat you think he or she has gotten.

Discussing only the subject at hand is a way of breaking down the complexities of domestic finance into small, manageable arenas. While you may want to cover several topics in one sitting, jump into only one at a time. Talk about savings, for example, until everything that needs to be said on the subject is said. Then move on.

3. Use reflective listening.

How many times do you really hear what your mate is saying? In the art of moneyspeak, knowing how to listen can be more important than knowing how to talk.

Most of us don't turn off our own simultaneous translators long enough to understand what is being said to us on its own terms. Instead, we reinterpret the information given, then react to our own interpretations. All too many money talks, in other words, sound like this exchange between Aaron and Camille:

AARON: *Whenever I look in the checkbook I never know where we stand.*

CAMILLE: *You're saying I spend too much money, aren't you?*

AARON: *No, I'm not. I just*

CAMILLE: *Go on, admit it. You think I spend too much!*

Reflective listening means, specifically, reflecting back to someone what you've heard him or her say. As Dr. Ellen McGrath, a highly respected marriage and family counselor with offices in both New York and California, points out, "It's not a process of simply replicating the words, but of hearing and acknowledging the emotional components of those words. You don't have to agree, assess, or react. Sometimes loved ones just want a compassionate and neutral listener."

After a little coaching on reflective listening, Aaron and Camille's checkbook conversation went more smoothly.

AARON: *I can never figure out what's going on when I look at the checkbook. I don't know how much is coming in or going out.*

CAMILLE: *It sounds like you're frustrated trying to figure out our checkbook and where our money is going. Am I right?*

AARON: *That's exactly what I'm saying. Can you explain some of these entries to me?*

CAMILLE: *Sure.*

In using reflective listening, Camille realized Aaron really was commenting on some confusion over the bookkeeping, not attacking her about her spending, as she at first presumed.

4. Stay with 'I' messages.

When you corner a cat, you should be prepared to get scratched. Similarly, when you verbally accuse your mate, you should expect a defensive comeback.

Moneyspeak messages that begin with 'you' (as in "You never pay the bills on time") are usually treated with suspicion and counterattack. In most cases they're verbal acts of war.

Instead, use 'I' messages whenever possible. Beginning sentences with 'I' (as in "I believe . . ." or "I'm worried about ") conveys a much different intention. 'I' messages are reflections of your own state of mind, not judgments about your mate's. They acknowledge a subjectivity in your viewpoint; that you're not making sweeping, all-knowing claims about your partner's behavior.

Saying "I feel frustrated that these books are such a mess" is vastly different from saying "You never keep the paperwork organized." Your partner will heartily appreciate the difference.

Watch out for 'you' messages disguised as 'I' messages. "I feel frustrated about our financial situation" is very different from "I feel you are irresponsible with money," even though both have the requisite 'I feel.'

5. Call for change and identify consequences.

Even the most open, collaborative-sounding moneyspeak isn't worth the time and trouble if measurable results aren't produced. The last step in focal communicating is to call for change. State the change you want to see in specific, finite terms. Then state a consequence that will happen if the change does not occur. After that, ask for agreement.

Aaron called for change this way: "I'd like for us to record all the checks we write at the moment we write them, and to spend half an hour each week together going over the checks and balancing the checkbook. If we don't do this, I'll keep feeling frustrated, you'll remain defensive, and we'll never know where we stand with our bank account. Will you agree to that, Camille?"

Every relationship that ever ended because of wholesale money differences did so because partners let too many small disagreements go by unresolved. The highest form of moneyspeak is communication as action—when talking about it is synonymous with doing something about it. Collisions and collusions have one thing in common: In their redundant and cyclical nature, they're unable to create lasting change. Collisions stir up too many hostilities; collusions bog down in too many lies.

The better you manage your money talk, the better you'll manage your money. Take a moment to reflect on the last exchange you had regarding money. Was it a collision, a collusion, or a collaboration? For the next week, bring up the subject of money several times, and practice focal communicating. I guarantee you will notice a positive difference. Effective moneyspeak always shows a profit.

Chapter FIVE

Money Meanings and Motivations

*Truth #5: What drew you together is often
the very thing that drives you apart.*

"**W**e agree on most things. We even have the same taste in
food and movies. When it comes to money, though, Robert and I
are on opposite sides of the universe," Nancy was saying as she
spiraled a strand of long blond hair around her index finger.

Robert laughed in agreement. "Say the word 'payday' to me and
I start thinking a night on the town, vacations in Mexico, new snow
skis—that kind of thing. Say the word to Nancy and she thinks rent
and electric bills."

Nancy and Robert were young, athletic California natives. They
had just moved in together and were finding themselves bickering
constantly over how to manage their small income.

"We're young," Robert continued. "I figure there's plenty of
time to get serious down the line. We should be out seeing the
world, having a ball. What I want out of this financial planning is to
figure a way I can do all that. I think money should be used for living it up."

"But, Robert, how on earth can you talk about seeing the world when the light bill still hasn't been paid?" said Nancy irritably. "I don't want to end up in my thirties paying for all the money mistakes I made in my twenties. We should be using our money to build a future. I'd like to see the world as much as anyone. But there are other priorities, too, like security."

Nancy and Robert had run aground in a common area of financial misunderstanding: the meaning of money.

To Nancy, a paycheck symbolized safety, comfort, and security; to Robert it was permission to venture out, to be stimulated by the new and exciting. It was as though they were American travelers in London who order biscuits for breakfast—and are surprised when they're served crackers! They were saying the right words, but getting the wrong results.

The Four Meanings of Money

If you asked twenty people what money means to them, you would get twenty different responses. When I've posed that question during speaking engagements, the answers come fast and furious: Trips to Tahiti. Kids' college tuition. Power. Sexiness. Tummy tucks. Freedom. And yes, even happiness.

Like opinions on the weather, everyone's got a notion about the true nature of money. Yet, no matter how different we are, there are significant similarities regarding the financial domain we share.

Hidden Investments, of course, shape our money personalities. Our individual quirks, biases, and beliefs cluster into primary themes—central motivations that govern how we use money. There are four primary money motivators:

- Freedom
- Security
- Power
- Love

While at different times in life you're influenced by all of these forces, usually one will prevail. It becomes your unconscious raison d'être, the unspoken reason you fight rush-hour traffic every morning. It subliminally rides herd over every love/money exchange.

Your primary need for freedom, security, power, or love sets the agenda every time you make a choice: from major life transitions (careers, lovers, lifestyles) to the smallest daily transactions (will you order the bargain lunch special or pay more and order a la carte?).

Mind you, these categories aren't hard and fast. The security-oriented have been known to drop a few dollars at the blackjack tables in Las Vegas. Power fiends occasionally give someone else a minute to speak.

Rather, like stock market indicators, primary money motivators illuminate preferred tendencies and predict trends. If you crave freedom above all else, for example, there's a high probability you will choose a week in Hawaii over a contribution to your IRA. Odds are good you don't even have an IRA.

How much balance you have in your life depends on how well you have mitigated the tendency to be 'one way' with the desire to be flexible and well rounded.

Discover Your Personal Money Motivations

A look at these primary money drives will give you important clues to your partner's behavior and your own. What does money mean to each of you? What sparks that urge to make or spend it? To fight about it?

Take a few minutes to complete this self-test. Write down the answer to these questions. Have your partner do the same.

1. Money is important because it allows me to...
    a. do what I want to do.
    b. feel secure.
    c. get ahead in life.
    d. buy things for others.

2. I feel that money...
    a. frees up my time.
    b. can solve my problems.
    c. is a means to an end.
    d. helps make relationships smoother.

3. When it comes to saving money, I...
    a. don't have a plan and don't often save.
    b. have a plan and stick to it.
    c. don't have a plan but manage to save anyway.
    d. don't make enough money to save.

4. If someone asks about my personal finances, I...
    a. feel defensive.
    b. realize I need more education and information.
    c. feel comfortable and competent.
    d. would rather talk about something else.

5. When I make a major purchase, I...
    a. go with what my intuition tells me.
    b. research a great deal before buying.
    c. feel I'm in charge—it's my/our money.
    d. ask friends/family first.

6. If I have money left over at the end of the month, I...
    a. go out and have a good time.
    b. put the money into savings.
    c. look for a good investment.
    d. buy a gift for someone.

7. If I discover I paid more for something than a friend did, I...
    a. couldn't care less.
    b. feel it's okay because I also find bargains at times.
    c. assume he spent more time shopping, and time is money.
    d. feel upset and angry at myself.

8. When paying bills, I...
    a. put it off and sometimes forget.
    b. pay them when due, but no sooner.
    c. pay when I get to it, but don't want to be hassled.
    d. worry that my credit will suffer if I miss a payment.

9. When it comes to borrowing money, I...
    a. simply won't—don't like to feel indebted.
    b. only borrow as a last resort.
    c. tend to borrow from banks or other business sources.
    d. ask friends and family because they know I'll pay.

10. When eating out with friends I prefer to...
    a. divide the bill proportionately.
    b. ask for separate checks.
    c. charge the bill to my bank card and have others pay me.
    d. pay the entire bill because I like to treat my friends.

11. When it comes to tipping, I...
    a. sometimes do and sometimes don't.
    b. Just call me Scrooge.
    c. resent it, but always tip the right amount.
    d. tip generously because I like to be well thought of.

12. If I suddenly came into a lot of money, I...
    a. wouldn't have to work.
    b. wouldn't have to worry about the future.
    c. could really build up my business.
    d. would spend a lot on family and friends and enjoy time
       with them more.

13. When indecisive about a purchase I often tell myself...
    a. it's only money.
    b. it's a bargain.
    c. it's a good investment.
    d. he/she will love it.

14. In my family...
    a. I handle all the money and pay all the bills.
    b. my partner takes care of the finances.
    c. I pay my bills and my partner does the same.
    d. we sit down together to pay bills.

For scoring: Count the number of times you responded with an 'a,' 'b,' 'c,' or 'd,' excluding questions 3, 4, and 7 (which are for your information only). Whichever letter you chose most frequently reveals your primary money motivation: a. freedom; b. security; c. power; and d. love.

After watching so many people take this test, I realized money motivators could predict behavior patterns as well as that elusive quality we call 'style.' Most people fall into one of the four money styles, which I've characterized the following way: Freewheeler (freedom), Hedger (security), Driver (power), and Relater (love). Let's take a closer look at those money styles.

If You Answered Mostly 'A'—You Are a *Freewheeler*, and You...

* see money as primarily a source of freedom.
* crave autonomy.
* relate to money as a source of thrills, chills, risks, big wins, big losses, unlimited access.
* are generous . . . but on your own terms.
* trade love, security, and even power in exchange for the options to go anywhere, do anything you want.
* are either very rich (having made your money in some nontraditional business that paid off big) or very poor (preferring even a beat-up late-model Dodge and Burger King dinners to the grind of an eight-hour workday).
* are a freelancer and soloist at heart. Commitments are hard for you.
* have probably never balanced a checkbook or devised a budget in your life—except when forced to by a non-Freewheeler.
* Common professions: commission sales of any kind; arts, music, or writing; any job offering travel, opportunity, and no time clocks.

If You Answered Mostly 'B'—You Are a *Hedger*, and You...

* see money as primarily a source of security.
* crave safety above all else; glorify the predictable and keep a safe distance from the unknown and unforeseen.
* equate money with stability, protection, and insurance: a roof overhead, food on the table, a buffer between you and the vagaries of tomorrow.
* are elated watching the value of your real estate property appreciate or your blue-chip utilities stock go up a point.
* tend to trust money more than people.
* invest in sure things and avoid risk with about the same verve as you avoid root canals.

- hold a steady job and spend that paycheck responsibly.
- hedge every money-making move with a countermove to protect.
- are best suited to relationships with few surprises; you like to know what you're coming home to.
- have a hard time passing up a bargain, freebie, or good deal.
- balance your checkbook to the penny.
- Common professions: corporate professions in labor or middle management; any job with a regular salary, job security, and insurance benefits.

If You Answered Mostly 'C'—You Are a *Driver*, and You...

- see money primarily as a source of power.
- tend to be obsessive about your work.
- see money as a passport to greater options, fame, admiration, control over resources and other people.
- want success and the status symbols it is measured by.
- like to be in control and are well adapted to management positions; as much as you drive others, you drive yourself harder.
- won't be happy until you're chairman of the board.
- are a loner; no one can quite keep up with you.
- are impatient, thorough, and to-the-point.
- detest vulnerability of any kind, and when it comes to a choice between family and career, home life finishes a distant second.
- make sure someone else balances your checkbook.
- pay attention to your budget only when you want to.
- Common professions: entrepreneurial ventures, head of companies, head of state; anything where there is competition and the thrill of the hunt.

If You Answered Mostly 'D'—You Are a *Relater*, and You...

- value friends and family above all else, and use money to enhance those relationships.

- are kind, understanding, motherly/fatherly, and consenting; a tireless listener—give, give, give. You can't resist an open hand.

- are the perennial nurturer, contributor, and volunteer.

- use money to make life a little better for friends and family.

- have probably used money to 'buy' love in the form of appreciation, attention, and acknowledgment.

- balance your checkbook—and everyone else's too.

- Common professions: housewife/househusband, nurse, teacher, counselor, doctor, philanthropist, saint; any job in the service industry.

Two Styles Under One Roof

Few people are so homogeneous and consistent that they exhibit only one style. You probably found your money traits in several of the groupings.

Just as there is never only one way, there are no perfect combinations. Few people are simply 'made for each other.' In relationships where both partners are fully expressing themselves, there will be magnetic reactions of both attraction and repulsion.

The attraction is what works in your relationship, the manner in which you complement each other's strengths and compensate for weaknesses.

The repulsion, however, is the source of your money fights. Let's look for a moment at the display of fireworks ignited when individuals with different money motivations come together. Which of the following scenarios is most like your own personal situation?

Scenario I

TODD: *Honey, why don't we stay home tonight. There's a couple of games on TV I'd like to see, and we really haven't spent much time together or with the kids lately.*

SHARON: *Not tonight. I have a stock market seminar down at the community college. Then I have to come back and prepare for that presentation I'm doing tomorrow. Sorry, but work is heavy right now—not much I can do about it.*

TODD: *You're a consenting adult. Your life won't be an utter failure because you stayed home one night. And I don't know why you keep looking for these crazy ways to invest our money. The kids are going to need it for school next year, and we had planned to send Mom and Dad on a little vacation—remember?*

SHARON: *I think you re forgetting something—that extra income came from the two big sales I made last month. I should be the one to decide where it will go.*

Profile

Todd (a Relater) is the consummate 'homebody'; bliss to him is a long night on a soft sofa with the wife and kids. Money is a means of feathering the family nest: more gifts under the Christmas tree, private schools for the kids. His goals are all directed toward loved ones. His self-esteem comes from being a good person, a solid parent, a faithful mate.

Sharon (a Driver) wants power, options, and upward mobility. Money to her is a means of furthering her ability to earn more money, in a quest for ever-higher status. She is driven and productive. She competes with everyone, even her spouse. Her goals are directed toward external achievements and stimulation. Self-esteem comes from effecting change in the world around her.

Problems

Todd lives in a perennial state of rejection, his own need to nurture left frustrated; Sharon feels harassed, bogged down by a husband who only grows more needy and weak as she expands her power and influence. He's threatened by the excitement she derives from the thrills of the marketplace; she's a bit out of touch with her own home life, oblivious to her children's projects or the broken dishwasher.

Potential

As an effective Driver, Sharon keeps the family's standard of living high as she maneuvers, strategizes, and charges her way to the top; Todd can keep the money issue balanced with the inner harmonies of home life—walks in the garden, long talks over breakfast. Sharon adds an adrenalized dose of excitement to the relationship, always exploring new possibilities. Todd makes sure the family's emotional needs are met with vacations at the lake and summer barbecues for friends. Sharon's negotating abilities serve the family well: She's a whiz at haggling with the landlord. Todd keeps her mercenary tendencies in check, reminding her that people count, too.

Scenario 2

> TAMARA: *Every one of our friends has had a party. We're the only ones who are invited over to other people's houses and never have anyone here. What is wrong with you? Really, Ed, you're the cheapest person I know.*
>
> ED: *It has nothing to do with being cheap. I just don't see the point in spending a lot of money on some party. The house gets trashed. And they're not that much fun*
>
> TAMARA: *Don't you ever want to do something for somebody else, just to do it? Because you like them? Or because you love them? If you really loved me, you'd know how important it is for me to entertain my friends.*
>
> ED: *You can love people all you want without spending good money on them. We don't even have enough for ourselves.*

Profile

Both Ed (the Hedger) and Tamara (the Relater) are happiest when money flows into the relationship. However, Ed wants to stash it away for the proverbial rainy day. Tamara wants to use it to draw friends and family closer. The two share a lot in common emotionally—they both value stability and predictability. They need security in their love relationships, and use money to get it.

Problems

While Tamara spends money on Ed, he will rarely spend it on her, saving it instead for basic needs. He condemns her constant contributing to others as overindulgent; she interprets his stinginess as a 'lack of love.'

Potential

Tamara can teach Ed that money spent on loved ones is money well-invested. He can teach her that there are ways to express love other than running up the phone bills and department store charge accounts. Since Relaters and Hedgers tend to be loyal, reliable mates, they make good collaborators and can work peacefully together toward mutual goals. Both are well adapted to family life and like to focus on the immediate environment of home and neighborhood.

Scenario 3

> LINDA: *Why do you insist on always spending money on yourself? We need new carpeting, and you buy yourself a computer. We need a family car, and you buy a Fiat. You are so damned selfish.*

> ROD: *God, I hate it when you get on my back about spending money. I wanted a sports car—so what? We'll get a station wagon when we get old. I say let's live now, while we're still young enough to enjoy it. As for the carpeting, to tell you the truth, it's not one of my great priorities in life.*

Linda (the Relater) isn't happy until all decisions are mutual 'family' decisions; she detests unilateral choices. All communication lines should be open. Everything—absolutely everything—affects Relaters personally: a forgotten birthday present is nearly grounds for divorce.

Rod (a Freewheeler) is a unilateral decision maker by instinct. It's not that he doesn't love Linda; it just never occurs to him to include her. He hates being called to task for his money habits, and is at his best living in blissful self-interest.

Problems

What a match! The Relater feels neglected and the Freewheeler feels trapped. To quench their thirst for freedom, Freewheelers frequently operate outside of their relationship. To Relaters, nothing should exist outside of the relationship—financial choices included.

Potential

The Relater balances the Freewheeler's impulsiveness with a sense of direction, commitment, and grounding things Rod has always avoided and, often, secretly longed for. The Freewheeler can teach the Relater not to give everything away, since her martyr tendencies do get the better of her; he teaches her a little enlightened self-interest. Relaters provide a soft place to land, while Freewheelers teach those Relaters the purpose of wings.

Scenario 4

KARA: *Did you see those brochures I left on the table? We can get a round-the-world ticket—if we fly standby—for what it costs for that ski vacation we take every year.*

ETHAN: *Those ski vacations serve a purpose, though, dear. Remember, we go with the other partners in my company. A lot of important business gets conducted on those chair lifts.*

KARA: *I'm not sure you're aware of the fact that there's an enormous world out there. I, for one, would like to see it. If you want to spend our only vacation of the year discussing price/earnings ratios in subzero weather with a bunch of business stiffs, that's your choice. But winter here is summer in Brazil, and I need a tan.*

To Kara (a Freewheeler), the price of freedom and adventure is never too high. In both love and money, she lives by her wits, always willing to up the ante in hopes of brighter futures. Money comes and goes; she can pursue it with the savvy of a street fighter or walk away content with nothing. She doesn't believe in dues to pay, trusting her own good fortune to help her reach her goals.

For Ethan (a Driver), entrepreneurial adventures provide the ultimate 'high.' Freedom means only the freedom to go higher on the ladder of power while those around him go lower. He, too, is independent—from everything but his own drives. When it comes to achieving his goals, he is relentless, plodding, and consistent.

Problems

The Freewheeler/Driver relationship is lit up with fireworks: He's the consummate controller; she abhors being controlled. She rides the wings of fate wherever they may take her. He is earth-bound, willing to move mountains to get where he's going. And he always knows where he's going. In his eyes, she's mercurial, irre-sponsible, and frivolous. To her, he's headstrong, boorish, insensi-tive and materialistic—a threat to her spontaneity and creativity.

Possibilities

The Freewheeler and the Driver have a lot to agree on. They both love to spend money. Their dynamic personalities are mag-netic, attracting the most interesting of life's prospects. Not bound by the mundane concerns of home and safety, they can shoot very high together (but must avoid the tendency to burn each other out).

Scenario 5

ELAINE: *So, are we going to buy the car or not? How many times are you going to go over this in your mind?*

FRED: *I just want to make sure we're doing the right thing. Interest rates may go up, so if we're going to buy, we should buy now. Then again, if they go down, I'll feel like an idiot for buying too soon. Also, what if we can't afford the payments down the line? There's a lot to consider.*

ELAINE: *Payments will take care of themselves. You never know—maybe we'll win the lottery. The only thing we need to consider is whether the car's going to be a four-door or a two-door; blue, red, or black.*

Elaine (a Freewheeler) and Fred (a Hedger) always end up at crosspurposes. She risks everything. He risks nothing. Elaine be-lieves details (like how the car will be paid for) handle themselves. She's intuitive, brave, whimsical. The predictable beckons with as much allure as a month at San Quentin. Fred surveys the territory before each move, like a chess player studiously weighing each op-tion. The choice of a new car is weighed against all other choices. Just as he needs to know the financial facts, he is meticulous in his measuring of the relationship, weighing how much love he's giving versus what he's received.

Problems

The Hedgers and the Freewheelers are natural adversaries: To her, he's timid, indolent, and cheap. To him, she's capricious, inconsistent, and the ultimate love/money liability.

He needs to put a toe in the water and wade in slowly. She dives into the deep end. Fred's a born saver. Elaine has refined spending to an art. When threatened emotionally, the Hedger uses money to insulate himself; for the Freewheeler, money buys a one-way ticket out.

In their most compulsive forms, Hedgers can be self-denying ("I can't buy that for myself") while the Freewheeler is dangerously self-indulgent ("Nothing is too good for me"). Fred needs proof of love and commitment. Elaine responds to his constant demands like a deer caught in a car's headlights—wishing only to break and run.

Potential

At its best, this is the perfect combination of security and excitement. Fred's responsible nature balances Elaine's flighty impetuousness. He can save her from her own roller coaster burn-out tendencies, while she can save him from stagnation.

Scenario 6

LEAH: *Now, Chris, you know we can't afford another franchise. You've already opened two this year. Our house payments are sky-high and we're already in a lot of debt. Why are you jeopardizing us like this? What if these franchises don't make it?*

CHRIS: *I have a business to run. How do you think we're paying for that house in the first place? Without these franchises, we'll always be two steps behind the competition. In this game, there's no second place.*

Profile

Leah (a Hedger) pulls back into safety at each of life's junctures. Making those house payments is crucial to her; not for love of hearth and home, but in worship of all things 'rock solid.' Everything new is a risk; every risk a threat to her survival. Chris (a Driver) keeps her at hysteria's edge with the risks he takes in his quick climb to the top. He responds to her overcautiousness with overzealousness, obliviously plowing through any obstacle in order to win.

Problems

Where Leah can be miserly, tentative, stubborn, and cowardly, Chris can be bullish, daring, insensitive, and single-minded. Leah lives in perpetual fear of the unknown while Chris relishes the unconquered precipice. The two come to blows at every new turn in the road, every time life presents a new challenge.

Potential

Leah can also be dependable, loyal, honest, and precise. Chris is strong and goal-oriented. The Hedger sees to details: paying the phone bill, checkbook balancing, taxes filing. The Driver can hold on to the long-range vision: keeping up their lifestyle, broadening horizons.

Same-Style Couples: The Truth About Birds of a Feather

So, all you have to do is partner up with someone just like yourself? Think of the possibilities! You'll agree on everything! You'll spend the same, save the same, and never have another fight. Yes? No.

Even when two like-styled lovers come together, the tendency to differ, to change points of view, to posture back and forth and shift attitudes is inevitable.

When two Freewheelers, Drivers, Hedgers, or Relaters meet at the altar, the union of like-minded souls doesn't guarantee love everlasting. Like familiarity, compatibility also breeds contempt. When two Hedgers decide to save money, one will save more. So prudent are they with their dollars, they compound their anxieties by agreeing on their fears.

Two Hedgers I once knew, convincing each other there would soon be a depression, put all of their investment money in gold bullion. I imagine they're still waiting for the hard times to come.

When two Freewheelers decide to spend, one will tend to spend more. They'll fight over what toys to buy from the Sharper Image catalogue: underwater radios or telephones for the shower?

Computerized exercycles or a miniature pool table? They egg each other on, and fight when economic realities catch up with them.

A client once complained to me that she felt her freewheeling style was cramped by her husband, a merciless spendthrift who kept them constantly in trouble with bill collectors. It fell upon her to be the responsible one, and she hated it.

In the union of two Relaters, one will be more nurturing than the other, give more gifts, cook more dinners, do more favors. They run the danger of being so consumed with getting their emotional needs met, there's little time for earning money. The lack of money, in turn, threatens their ability to give to others. Christmas was a nightmare for two Relaters I knew. Each spent months in the malls trying to find gifts that would outdo the presents of the previous year.

When both partners seek power, they will compete with each other and jockey for position. Who is busier? Whose job is more important? Each will try to get a leg up on the other. A famous agent in Hollywood once divorced his actress wife because he couldn't stand it that she made more money and was better connected than he.

It isn't hard to see that what drew you together is often the very thing that drives you apart. You are attracted to those qualities and skills of your partner that you don't possess, then spend the rest of your time together rebelling against those same qualities and skills.

Think of the primary money motivators that have come together in your relationship. What are the problems you see? What is the potential? Discuss those problems and potentials with your partner.

Finding harmony in your love/money relationship, then, is not a matter of fitting both of you into the same mold. You're ahead of the game when you admit your partner's money motivations may not match yours exactly. Respecting differences in perception and needs is the first step in creating common ground where love and money can meet on peaceful terms.

Money is a limited resource. As we all know, it never really buys lasting freedom, security, love, and power, but only a temporary facsimile of those states. To feel really free, secure, loving, and powerful requires emotional maturity, an integrated sense of personal value money cannot buy.

PART TWO

Where Do We Go From Here?

"What does all this psychological stuff have to do with why we screw up our budget and fight about the phone bill?" you might be asking. "How do we reconcile our differences when they show up as money fights?"

The first half of this book introduced you to your psychological portfolio. Now you have taken the first five steps toward looking at beliefs about money, gender roles, power, communication, and habits in a new, more informed way.

The Hidden Investments you have discovered constitute the *why's* of money behavior—why you feel, act, and react the way you do. It's now time to look at the *when's*—the specific instances when your combined psychological portfolios sabotage (or enhance) your shared financial life.

When couples come into my office they bring with them two file folders. One contains all the bank statements, tax returns, insurance information, net worth, cash flow statements—everything we can lay out on the table and touch, organize and quantify. The other folder, just as important, is the one we cannot see. It is nonetheless real. It holds the hopes, dreams, fears, concerns, positive and negative experiences about money that all of us have. The prevailing purpose of this book is to integrate those two folders so that they make sense, reduce conflict and build financial independence. Let's face it, a marriage relationship these days is an economic partnership as well as an emotional one. Just try divorce and tell me this isn't so!

When it comes right down to it, we have money fights with our spouses because we're different from them. From what I've observed, those differences in handling money fall into five general areas.

Each area or 'dimension' of difference has its own dynamic. It's easier to see that dynamic by using continuum diagrams. Like a color wheel that shows the infinite number of colors between black and white, continuums show the kinds of money management behavior possible between two polar extremes.

All couples encounter these five dimensions of differences from time to time—and handle such encounters with varying degrees of harmony.

The Couples Continuum:
Dimensions of Individual Differences

Spending..Saving
SPEND/SAVE

Risk Affinitive ....Risk Aversive
RISK ACCEPTANCE LEVEL

Generalist ....Particularist
ORGANIZATIONAL STYLE

Impulsive .... Reflective
DECISION-MAKING STYLE

Change Adaptive...Change Avoiding
FLEXIBILITY

Few people are on the extreme right or extreme left of these spectrums. If you've been operating with any degree of success, you are probably somewhere in the middle ground. Nor is your position on these lines fixed in cement. At one stage in life you may be very dependent on your mate, growing more independent over time. Or vice versa.

Where you think you are on a continuum isn't necessarily where your partner sees you. You may consider yourself a modest risk-taker while your mate may think you're a peril-happy fool.

Sometimes I ask clients to plot their own positions and those of their spouses on the continuum line. What they come up with shows how different perceptions of the same financial behavior can be. For example, when I asked Brad and Courtney to plot their spending and saving patterns by putting their initials on the continuum, they were surprised by the results.

Brad and Courtney's Spend/Save Habits:

Brad's viewpoint:

Her	Him	

Spending..Saving

Courtney's viewpoint:

Her   Him

Spending..Saving

According to Brad, Courtney was shop-happy, while he saw himself as a methodical spender and saver ruled by moderation. Courtney maintained she had healthy spending habits that dipped toward the excessive only occasionally. Brad, on her continuum, showed up as an out-and-out miser.

Take a moment to consider where you and your mate sit on each of the six continuums. Ask your partner where he or she believes your money behavior fits. The results will be telling.

The Pas de Deux of Love and Money

It's important to realize your money behavior will change, not just over time but also in relationship to the actions and attitudes of your partner.

Love/money relationships are ongoing dances. Sometimes you're in step with each other, at other times you careen toward opposite ends of the floor. Sometimes you compensate for your differences and come together, at other times you polarize and drift apart. These laws of compensation and polarization are fundamental and deserve a closer look.

Compensation

Partners initially deal with their differences by compensating for each other. The spouse of an avid spender, for example, may try to save a little here and there as a last line of defense against the bill collectors. One lovingly tries to balance the excesses of the other.

Polarization

Compensating behavior leads to polarization. Eventually the compensation game grows tiresome and lines are drawn. Slowly, partners become more entrenched in opposing corners. He spends; she saves. She nags about his spending; he spends more. He calls her a cheapskate; she hoards even more. Soon they're headed at warp speed toward opposite ends of the spectrum.

Polarization is what's happening when you find yourselves moving further apart, fighting more ferociously about subjects that, at one time, were not even important issues to you.

"He/she was never like this before we got married," bewildered partners often complain when they find themselves sleeping next to someone who is fast becoming unrecognizable.

So how do you come back from the brink?

In the chapters that follow we'll be answering that question as we explore each dimension of love/money difference. I'll introduce you to couples entangled in situations I know will be familiar to you.

Along the way I'll offer techniques and solutions for you to try. Some are strictly financial in nature, planning tools addressing the particular problems of couples. While it was never my intention to turn you into a Wall Street investment wizard, you will find in the following pages all the elements of basic fiscal fitness.

Other techniques address problems and needs of the psychological portfolio: How to mediate differences, overcome bad habits, and broaden horizons.

Use them, and the polarized differences you now see as breaking points in your relationship can become balancing points where hearts, minds, and money can meet.

Chapter SIX

Where Does the Money Go?

Truth #6: It's not what you make but what you keep that counts.

"**W**hen I got home from work that day, I couldn't believe my eyes," said Daniella. "A brand-new computer was sitting there on the desk, with the screen glowing at me. Each component had an invisible price tag. When I tallied it up—all hell broke loose.

"I screamed at Josh for half an hour. How could he do this to me—to us? He knew we were saving up to buy a house. We'd been discussing for months how much we'd have to save for the down payment. Then he went out and bought a computer with all the money we'd saved. It sent us back to square one."

"What were your reasons, for buying the computer?" I asked Josh, who by now looked decidedly uncomfortable. "I never wanted to hurt Daniella," Josh replied. "I was just fed up with working so hard for my money and not getting to spend any of it on myself. Every extra dime went to the down payment on the house.

"I wondered if I even wanted such a big responsibility. We'd have to save so much money, and go without a lot of the things we really enjoy—like restaurants, nice clothes, and, for me, electronic equipment. When I was single I never deprived myself of anything. I'd been wanting a new computer for a long time. When I saw it advertised on sale, I figured what the hell. We'll make up the money somehow."

Spending the Dollars You Share

These are the most volatile questions of today's money relationships:

- What will we spend our money on?

- How will we save those precious resources?

- Whose priorities are more important or more valid?

- When we spend, will it be for my dreams or yours?

- How can we manage our money effectively when one of us saves/spends compulsively?

Like Daniella and Josh, we all want to live 'the good life.' And we all have different definitions of what the good life means. For some, a comfortable house, a functional car, and a little extra loot stowed away for tomorrow will do nicely. Others won't stop until they're sipping champagne in Europe.

How you spend and save reflects your deepest personal values, your dreams, and what you think is important. How you manage your cash flow can also expresses how deeply you value your relationship or stand up for your individuality within it.

Some couples enter financial marriage perfectly in sync with each other's habits. Others have a harder time of it. Some marriages go awry when both partners overspend and have to keep bailing each other out. Or when one likes to spend and the other likes to save, and they suffer from their differences. Or when both agree money needs to be salted away but clash over how much to save and where to invest.

I've also met couples who swear they never openly fight about where their money will go, yet they answer "no" to these questions:

1. Do we have enough money to support our current life-style?

2. Are we increasing our wealth in a way that keeps up with inflation and moves us closer to our long-term goals?

3. Do we have a consistent savings and investment strategy?

4. Do we know where our money goes?

5. Do we usually agree on how money should be spent and saved?

Ask yourself those same questions. If you answered "no" to any of them, your spending and saving patterns beg for a change.

Sometimes my job as a financial planner is simply to restate the obvious. You probably already know what it takes to manage money well: spend less than you earn and wisely save or invest what's left over. As you also know, that sounds a lot easier than it is.

Directing cash flow, instead of being swept along in its currents, demands that you take an active stance toward your finances rather than a reactive one. Is your relationship profit-driven or expense-driven?

If it's profit-driven, you plan ahead, save, and make sure your money is working for you. If it's expense-driven, you live enslaved by your bills and use your energies to keep up with obligations, rather than funding mutual dreams.

The goal for most of us is financial independence—that point at which we have enough investments generating income so that we no longer work by necessity but by choice.

Yet partners with different psychological portfolios will manage their financial portfolios differently. They hold their own standards for what financial independence means, and travel divergent paths to get there. To help couples resolve spending and saving differences, I usually have three tasks:

✓ To point out where each partner perceives they are on the continuum of spending and saving, and to build a bridge of understanding between them.

✓ To spot problems in both their financial and psychological portfolios (binge spending, for example) and suggest ways to stop habits that don't work and cultivate ones that do.

✓ To pinpoint where priorities diverge, those legitimate areas where partners simply want and need different things. I then try to forge a compromise so that individual goals can be met, and the relationship can still be kept intact.

"My husband can't hold onto a dollar to save his life." "My wife is so cheap she squeaks." When individuals complain to me about the spending or saving behavior of their partners, these are the extremes they portray (as on the continuum). Let's look at what's behind this behavior.

Spending...Saving

SPEND/SAVE

Profile of a Spender

Spenders feel their power, self-determination, and excitement from disbursing money and accumulating goods. Shopping is synonymous with stroking; it perks up their self-image and rewards them for work well done. In the form of gift-giving, spending money is a gesture of love and acknowledgment.

Spending veers toward danger when spenders spend to overcome depression ("When the going gets tough, the tough go shopping"), or to nurture themselves by using material goods as surrogates for a deeper sense of self-love and reward. If you are, or your partner is, an addicted spender, you buy

- what you don't need (or sometimes even want).
- when there is not enough money.
- without sensitivity to the needs of your family, friends, or personal financial integrity.

Profile of a Saver

Savers exhibit self-determination by accumulating wealth and saying a self-disciplined "no" to life's extraneous luxuries. They prefer the slow building of financial clout and capital to the fleeting thrill of a spending spree.

Addictive saving, however, is as insidious and destructive as overspending. The miser squirrels pennies for the mere sake of watching them accumulate. Saving becomes an end in itself.

Money, to the chronic saver, is not an investment in future happiness. There is always another tomorrow when the money will be better spent—and even that tomorrow never comes. If you are, or your partner is addicted to saving, you save

- while depriving yourself and your loved ones of the material pleasures—even necessities—your money was meant to buy.

- instead of translating financial riches into any other kind of assets or investments with growth potential.

- to fill an inner emotional bank account that is never deemed full; security is always just out of reach.

What's Going On

Most spending and saving patterns come from deeply held Hidden Investments that surface as urges for love, security, power, or freedom. It's a rare financial choice that is psychologically neutral.

There were good reasons why Josh drained the savings account to buy the computer—a chain of 'logical' reactions that led him to that choice.

There were also good reasons why that choice sent Daniella careening off the emotional deep end. To get closer to the source of Daniella and Josh's problems, I began asking questions.

"How was money handled in your families?" I asked.

Daniella's early money memories were vivid and she bristled as she spoke. "We moved around a lot—mostly to stay away from bill collectors. My dad had a new job, in a new city, every year. There was never even a home to rely on, we were evicted so many times. I grew up longing to have a stable base—house, kids, a familiar neighborhood. When Josh bought that computer, all I could think was 'Here I go, living on the brink of disaster again.'"

"At least you got to see new places and meet new people," Josh interjected. "My family was so stable we all nearly died of boredom. We never went anywhere. My parents didn't even go out for dinner. Man, I swore I'd never be roped and tied to the middle-class dream like they were. That's why I've always kept life simple. My motto has always been 'Keep overhead low and be able to move out quickly.'"

"It's clear to me you both brought some strong Hidden Investments from your early family life into your present relationship," I said. "Do you realize how much the memories of your parents, how they lived and handled money, are driving you in your behavior with each other?"

"I see it," said Daniella, "but those aren't easy memories to do away with. It was a very painful period. My father was such a god-awful provider. I can't tell you how many nights I dreamed he would go away and Mom would marry a man like the father in *Father Knows Best*. What's amazing is, I fell in love with Josh. Parts of him are so much like my dad, I could scream."

"I know what Daniella's saying. Most of the time I look at her and see the strong, independent woman that she is. But buying this house has brought out a side of her that's like my own mom—you know, nagging a lot and sacrificing everything for the house and family. When I see that in her, I get claustrophobia."

"You are a Hedger, Daniella, and you, Josh, are a Freewheeler," I explained. "For as long as you're together you'll always spend and save money differently. Which is why the lines of communication between you have to be exceptionally clear.

"Can you think of a way to let each other know how you're feeling when those fears of scarcity and feelings of claustrophobia first begin to surface?"

Josh wrinkled his forehead. "I suppose I could have told Daniella how antsy I was getting from all the restrictions. If she knew how bad I was feeling, maybe she could have helped me figure out a way to buy the computer without emptying the savings account."

"That would have changed everything," said Daniella. "I don't mind altering plans. I just hate it when plans change and I have no control over the outcome. If we had talked this way months ago, maybe all this wouldn't have happened."

"I'm going to ask you something now, and I want you to answer truthfully," I said. "Do you both really want the house?"

"Yes," they replied in unison.

"Knowing what you know about your feelings, is there a way to get the house without causing resentments?"

We came up with a solution that sat well with both. They agreed to put money into savings toward the house each month, but not every extra dime. 'Fun money' was set aside to satisfy Josh's need to cut loose financially. When his spending no longer threatened Daniella's base-line security, she got to liking those extra dollars, too.

When Money Is Out of Control

Knowing why you are the way you are with your cash flow is different from taking paper in hand and doing something about it. First, you have to uncover what, precisely, is going wrong.

The Binge/Splurge Cycle

We've all been there:

"There's plenty of money here—let's spend," you say on some bright day when the consumer world beckons with pricey glory.

Then reality descends like a curtain of gloom. "Oh, God, we're broke. Batten down the hatches. No money leaves this house!"

Like compulsive eating, binge spending is inevitably followed by binge saving. At best, the cycle maintains an uneasy status quo: occasional bounced checks and irate creditors, but no serious financial damage.

At its worst, bingeing and splurging depletes the energy of your relationship in its constant cycle of drama, excess, and upset. The giddy joys of unbridled spending are followed by crashing financial hangovers, where the mere sight of the checkbook balance is excruciating. In the midst of this frenzy, there's little time for attaining real security or mutual goals.

Waiting for Good Luck

Some people are blessed (or cursed) with a gift for creating instant money miracles. If they need $100 on Wednesday, someone comes along on Tuesday with an unexpected check. They hang on the edge of trouble by their fingernails, and manage to pull themselves up at the very last minute.

In an old television show called *The Millionaire*, a character named Michael Anthony, who worked for an eccentric tycoon, would select people apparently at random, arrive on their doorsteps, and give them a million dollars.

Most people, in their wildest dreams, wait for Michael Anthony. The fantasy of sudden windfalls and strokes of financial luck is nearly universal. It is why we play the lottery and enter sweep-stakes.

I've had clients who live their financial lives counting on the last-minute save. Trusting fortune to bless you with rent money every month is dangerous and the odds aren't good. Fortunes change in an instant.

Plastic Mania and Debt Traps

More and more couples walk into my office every day with co-lossal amounts of debt, mainly in the form of credit card charges. Quadruple-digit balances seem to be as much a part of life in the fast lane as BMW's and beach houses.

In the past few decades, credit cards have opened up new, fertile ground for spenders. They offer a socially sanctioned and nearly irresistible way of spending money you don't have. Whereas the fiscally responsible use credit to float money and consolidate purchases, spenders use it for one thing only: to live beyond their means.

To the vulnerable or the uninitiated, credit looks like 'free money.' A $3,000 credit limit means 3,000 unclaimed dollars floating adrift in the financial universe. How tempting it is to forget about the bill coming down the line.

I think the responsible use of credit and debt is one of today's great challenges. With the American Dream soaring beyond most people's income, it's only too tempting to take that fatal bite of the credit apple.

Then woe unto you afterward. You'll be paying for that lunch you couldn't afford yesterday—but charged anyway—for many to-morrows to come.

Spending, Saving and Bridging the Gap

Playing Opposites

"I don't know where I go wrong with my spending," Josh once said to me. "I'm just so used to my habits, I don't even see them anymore. I only see the damage once it's done."

Not only do we not catch our own bad habits before we act, we also fail to see value in our partner's attitudes. A technique I use to help clients intervene in their own excesses is called 'playing opposites.'

If You're a Spender

This week operate as though you were a saver. Each day:

❏ Determine how much you will spend so money will be left over.

❏ Question whether each item you buy represents the best use of that money. Ask yourself, "Of all the things I could buy with this money, is this what I really want?" You'll find yourself saying 'no' to the spending impulse more often. At the end of the week, deposit what's left over in a savings account.

❏ Take an inventory: How does it feel to be a saver? Would you like to continue to be a saver? Discuss with your spouse ways that conserving resources might help your relationship.

If You're a Saver

Operate for the next week as though you were a spender:

❏ Buy one thing—something you don't necessarily need but want anyway—every day.

❏ Allow your partner to handle all the savings, so you can learn to hand over the financial reins and to trust your partner.

❏ Look at each dollar you have saved up until now and ask yourself, "To what material end (a home, happy retirement, etc.) will that dollar go?"

❏ Take an inventory: How does it feel to be a spender? Would you like to continue being a spender? Discuss with your spouse ways that sharing and disbursing resources might help your relationship.

Josh and Daniella completed this exercise and had dramatic shifts in attitude to report. "By playing the role of saver, I got to see what Daniella liked about saving money," said Josh. "It's really a mind game. The world offers you a million ways to spend money. The fun is finding ways around the system, to watch the bucks accumulate where you want them to."

"I played spender for the week—and, boy, did I have fun," Daniella enthused. "For once, I didn't have to nag Josh. I gave myself complete permission. I wouldn't want to keep up those spending habits—we'd never have a house of our own—but the game sure loosened me up."

Breaking the Credit Habit

Breaking the credit habit can be so difficult that sometimes the only way to arrest the hand-to-card response is by going cold turkey. If one of you tends toward 'plastic abuse,' request that the abuser hand over the credit cards to the other for safekeeping until all outstanding balances are paid. If both of you collude as abusers, give your cards to a friend.

If you use credit, understanding the benefits and the dangers will help you spend responsibly:

Credit Benefits
Good identification
Safe substitute for cash
Automatic record-keeping
Consolidates many purchases into one payment
Saves money when you can take advantage of a good sale
Orders can be placed by mail or phone
Provides leverage against merchants when problems arise

Credit Dangers
Constant temptation to overspend
Tendency to purchase non-essential items
Impulsive spending increases
 Payments are late or only partially made

Try not to Borrow at Interest Except . . .
When buying real estate
In dire emergency

Accumulate Cash Instead.

Budgets Don't Work—Cash Flow Management Does

Budgets are like diets. The minute you go on one, all you can think about is the things you can no longer have. Inevitably, when conscience imposes celery sticks and cottage cheese, all you crave is Haagen-Dazs ice cream and Mrs. Fields cookies. Budgets seem to aid and abet the binge/splurge cycles rather than create balance and flexibility in your cash flow.

To declare "I will spend only $300 on groceries every month" is to set up a failure every month you spend $400. Budgets, as they've been used in traditional financial planning, are arbitrary restrictions on spending. They are violated all too easily—especially when two partners try to share the same restrictions.

Resentments *always* crop up. Who spent more on entertainment? Who got to buy more clothes? When there is no way to reconcile individual and mutual expenditures, budgets will only give you something else to fight about.

As an alternative to such strait jacket financial planning methods, the His/Hers Cash Flow Management (CFM) system I've tailored for couples is a thumbnail sketch of both ideal and actual spending/saving habits. It gives partners responsibility for their individual inflows and outflows, all within the context of a partnership. It's a system based on documented financial experience rather than a pie-in-the-sky ideal of 'what you should spend.' Josh and Daniella did a spreadsheet on the computer and this is what their CFM statement looks like:

Last Quarter Average: Josh & Daniella								
OUTGO	JANUARY			FEBRUARY			MARCH		
	His	Hers	Joint	His	Hers	Joint	His	Hers	Joint
Fixed:									
Savings/Investments (to downpayment)			200			200			200
Rent			1,000			1,000			1,000
Insurance/auto	80	90		80	90		80	90	
Taxes	900	500		900	500		900	500	
Car payment	220	80		220	80		220	80	
Insurance/health			150			150			150
*Health club	40	40		40	40		40	40	

OUTGO	JANUARY			FEBRUARY			MARCH		
	His	Hers	Joint	His	Hers	Joint	His	Hers	Joint
Variable:									
Utilities			120			120			120
Groceries			300			250			350
*Clothing	220	78		120	50		60	-0-	
Telephone			80			53			69
Repair/Auto	93	-0-		-0-	112		-0-	-0-	
Auto/Gasoline	70	75		81	79		85	83	
*Restaurants	90	59	120	50	35	90	86	50	112
*Entertainment	80	36	150	150	48	110	120	52	125
Individual Purchases (computer, etc.)	20	15	32	980	25	-0-	-0-	17	36
Gifts/charities	20	36	40	60	40	100	-0-	42	86

Current Month's Projected Expenses									
	Three-Month Average			Pay Period April 1-15			Pay Period April 16-30		
	His	Hers	Joint	His	Hers	Joint	His	Hers	Joint
INCOME				1,450	1,050		1,450	1,050	
OUTGO *Fixed:*									
Savings/Investments (to downpayment)			200			100			100
Rent			1,000			1,000			
Insurance/auto	80	90		80				90	
Taxes	900	500		900	500				
Car payment	220	80			80		220		
Insurance/health			150						150
*Health club	40	40					40	40	150

	Three-Month Average			Pay Period April 1-15			Pay Period April 16-30		
OUTGO	His	Hers	Joint	His	Hers	Joint	His	Hers	Joint
Variable:									
Utilities			100			100			
Groceries			300			150			
*Clothing	113	43					*75	*50	
Telephone			67						67
Repair/Auto	31	37					31	37	
Auto/Gasoline	79	78		40	40		39	39	
*Restaurants	99	48	107	*30	*25	*52	*30	*25	*40
*Entertainment	116	45	128	*25	*25	*50	*25	*25	*50
Individual Purchases ('Fun' money, computer,etc.)	333	19	22	*25	*25	-0-	*25	*25	-0-
*Gifts/charities	26	39	75	*35	*35	-0-	-0-	-0-	*75
TOTAL EXPENSES PER PAY PERIOD	2,057	1,020	2,149	1,135	730	1,452	485	331	632

* Amounts noted with asterisk (*) are adjusted in the scheduling to conform to income and mutual agreement (Josh agreed not to buy any more computer components and to reduce money for clothes and entertainment. Daniella could therefore spend more).

Together Josh and Daniella make $5,000 a month. Previously their expenses exceeded their income by $226 a month. Under the new schedule, total expenses are $4,765. Therefore, additional savings per month of $235 were targeted for a new house. Seeing the high tax payments each made was an added incentive to purchase a home in order to get mortgage interest deductions and save on their taxes.

The His/Hers Cash Flow Management System

To create your own His/Hers CFM system, follow these simple steps. This exercise may take some time and patience, but you'll be rewarded with a clear overview of how resources flow through your marriage.

Step 1: Determine monthly expenditures by averaging three months of data.

❏ Sit down with your checkbook, credit card statements, and any other documentation of your inflow and outflow of money during the last three months.

❏ Do a spreadsheet on the computer or take a piece of ledger paper and divide it into four columns, the first titled OUTGO and the remaining three bearing the names of the last three months. Further subdivide those columns under HIS, HERS, and JOINT (See p. 115).

❏ Under OUTGO list fixed expenses (rent, insurance, car) and variable expenses (food, clothing, utilities). *Note with an asterisk which expenses are discretionary—that is, expenses you *choose* to incur rather than have to incur. Be honest about the difference between luxury and necessity.

Step 2: Project this month's cash flow based on past expenses.

❏ Take a clean sheet of ledger paper and divide it, too, into four columns: the first titled OUTGO, the second titled THREE-MONTH AVERAGE, the third titled with the dates of the first pay period of this month (for example, APRIL 1-15), the fourth titled with the dates of this month's second pay period (APRIL 16-30). Further subdivide those columns into HIS, HERS, and JOINT.

❏ Take your three-month flow chart and compute the average of each expense. (For example, if groceries cost $300 in January, $250 in February, and $350 in March, the average amount spent on groceries is $300.)

❏ On your current month's chart, list again all expenses under OUTGO and schedule in the average amount due on each expense under the appropriate pay period to see clearly when each bill is due. Total each column. Then add HIS, HERS, and JOINT subtotals for each pay period together to get your 'joint outgo.'

❑ You now know what you 'usually' spend each month, both separately and together. You also know your projected expenses for this month.

Step 3: Adjust income to expenses.

❑ Below each 'joint outgo' total, enter the amount of your take-home income for each pay period. If you live off one income, note that amount. If you both have incomes, note each individually, then add the total gross income.

❑ Compare the amount of income to the amount of outgo.

❑ If income is always more than outgo, then enter the amount of difference in your expense category called SAVINGS/INVESTMENT.

❑ If outgo is consistently more than income, look at the expenses you previously marked with an asterisk (your discretionary expenses). Discuss with your spouse which are 'his' luxuries, which are 'hers,' and which ones you share. If you disagree on which expenses to give priority to, note each expense on a three-by-five card and shuffle. Discuss each item and reprioritize the cards so that each spouse gets some luxuries, but not at the expense of necessities.

❑ Based on the agreements you made about discretionary expenses and adjust amounts so that your outflows conform to your inflows. (For example, Josh chose to reduce his spending on clothing, entertainment, and of course, computers; Daniella got to spend a little more in those areas than she had been averaging.)

❑ You now know what you may spend, given your projected income. You also know what role each of you will play in the ebb and flow of your mutual monies.

❑ When all of Josh and Daniella's spending and saving habits were finally down in irrefutable black-and-white, they could see the inequities in their relationship. Josh had been spending far more on discretionary items than Daniella. Daniella was resenting Josh without precisely knowing why. The computer was simply the last infraction.

❑ By making some thoughtful changes they were able to make an even larger deposit toward the house down payment, while still siphoning off 'fun money' for the immediately gratifying pleasures.

The Psychology of Saving

"I'm running against the clock," explained John, a forty-year-old computer software writer. "Lately, I've been taking things much more seriously. My parents are getting older and may need me to take care of them. I have a wife and two children, and about ten earning years left. I want to retire early so I need to start making provisions for the future."

For most couples (especially the young), keeping the financial ship afloat is stressful enough. Who has time to think about the future? It's hard to ponder such distant realities as long-term goals and retirement when you're working as hard as you can to keep up with your current expenses.

Life planning is one of the most emotionally rewarding and psychologically comforting processes you can do together. And life planning means saving money.

There are two truths in the psychology of saving money:

- *There is never a convenient time to save.* Just as your senses are drawn to the chocolate cake in the buffet line faster than they are to the steamed squash, so, too, you'll find more emotionally gratifying places to put money than burying it in a bank account.

- *Your expenses will expand to fit the size of your paycheck.* Isn't it funny how that happens? How often have you deluded yourself into thinking your saving habits will improve as soon as your income goes up? Left to your normal human devices, the more money you get, the more new expenses you'll invent—all while your savings go neglected.

Begin saving now. There are a variety of savings and investment instruments your financial planner can suggest. Trick your mind into holding on to money by treating savings as a billed expense. Actually pay yourself first, before you pay the rent and the electric bill. Most important, regard those savings as untouchable. Help each other obey the rules you set.

We've covered a lot of material in this chapter, some of it technical, other parts emotionally confronting. Understand this: Reconciling your portfolios in the areas of spending and saving is the most formidable challenge you will face in balancing love and money.

Begin facing that challenge now. In your relationship, who is the spender and who the saver? How might your partnership benefit from the ideas and exercises we've covered? Think of one spending/saving problem you've stumbled upon this last week. Use Cash Flow Management to help solve it.

It's not what you make, it's what you keep that counts. Your relationship is your best resource for helping you to strike a harmonious balance between spending and saving—and nothing resolves debates over the destiny of your resources more satisfyingly than money in the bank. Nothing.

Chapter SEVEN

Making It Past the Breaking Points: From Risk to Reward

Truth #7: You have to take the right risks to earn the best returns.

"What do you mean you want to take out a second mortgage so you can start a new construction company?" Corine asked, her hysteria barely suppressed. "You know how unstable the building industry is. We could lose our house! Our credit! All of it! How could you risk everything we've worked so hard for—again? Haven't you learned your lesson?"

"And how can you be so shortsighted?" David retorted bitterly. "I have as much talent as the guy I'm working for. Probably more. I know I'd be successful. Sure, there's some risk involved, but I can handle it. This industry is booming. If I'm going to make my move I'll have to do it now. You're just going to have to trust me."

During the years Corine and David had been my clients, I'd heard the same conversation more times than I could count. The proposed investments changed regularly, but the dynamic was always identical: David would wax euphoric over some sensational new business idea while; Corine would insist he was out of his mind.

David had made and lost all his money several times over. A building contractor most of his adult life, he put all the money he could pry away from Corine into investments. He liked nothing better than to take risks in hopes of seeing a big payoff. Every other month there was some new stock he knew would go through the roof, a new invention, or some real estate venture he swore would make him rich. The results, thus far, had been decidedly mixed.

Corine spent the early years of her marriage watching in disbelief as their standard of living soared and plummeted, depending on the vagaries of each new deal. "Living on this roller coaster is driving me crazy," she told me then. "I come from a stable family. I'm not used to this feast-or-famine way of life."

Risky Business

Risk. It's there every time you step into your car, buy a stock, or open your own business. It's also there whenever you make a serious investment in love.

To get married is to create a legally binding partnership that makes you responsible, emotionally and financially, for every money move your partner makes. Even long-term live-in relationships aren't exempt from that responsibility.

Unless some legal boundaries are established beforehand, you take on at the altar the benefits of your partner's future assets and the burden of future liabilities. His failing business becomes her red ink. Her debt to the Internal Revenue Service becomes his trouble with Uncle Sam.

"I wish we could have a terrific, romantic relationship, but one where I'm not liable for all his debts and goofball schemes," Corine once said to me.

As I told her, to be in love is to be liable to some degree. And to have a financial partnership that works is to minimize that liability and to work and risk together, as a team.

When an individual's basic survival is at stake, teamwork isn't always a cakewalk. Perceptions of risk vary incredibly. 'Fool's gold' to one spouse might be a 'sure thing' to the other. Committing those mutually owned dollars, with unresolved differences in risk tolerance, can be an investment in disaster.

Most relationships have their own silent systems of checks and balances that keep risk within manageable limits. Typically, one partner will play 'gambler' to the other's 'cautionary counselor.'

Those roles aren't always visible to outsiders. Many a financial planner has had the unfortunate experience of 'closing' on a deal, based on the more vocal partner's approval of it, only to have it fall through because the silent spouse registered a not-so-silent opposition once out of the office.

The goal in financial planning is to use risk intelligently for profit. In money, as in exercise, there's no gain without a little pain. Generally, the higher the risk, the higher the potential reward. Conversely, the lower the risk, the less money you stand to make. There are no risk-free investments. Even a portfolio of long term treasuries* declines in value when interest rates rise.

We know that every financial portfolio is a reflection, in dollars, of the investors' psychological portfolio—the money messages and memories, gender differences, power dynamics and money styles that create risk behavior.

Love/money partnerships that work always honor the risk threshold of each partner. Between the ultraconservative and the superaggressive, between unbridled financial recklessness and utter financial stagnation, is a level of risk that's right for both.

Most investment behavior falls in the middle range between risk aversion and risk affinity. Look for a moment at these extremes on the continuum we call Risk Acceptance Level, or RAL for short.

---

* Treasuries, long term – these are government-issued debt obligations of 1 year or longer. You can loan your government money and they will pay you interest. It is done through Treasury Bills, Bonds and Notes.

Risk Affinitive...**Risk Aversive**
RISK ACCEPTANCE LEVEL

Profile of the Risk Affinitive

The risk affinitive are robust investors. "No guts, no glory" is their motto. They are aggressive, dynamic, and action-oriented, happiest when living on the edge. Driven by the promise of big returns, they take on financial life as they do any other game with a big jackpot.

Money is perceived as a 'flow,' a renewable resource that will come, go, and come again many times in their lives. Unlike the risk aversive, who view each financial event as grimly significant, the risk affinitive see each risk as a mere event in a much larger game.

Sublimely confident in their own ability (sometimes too confident), the risk affinitive dabble in entrepreneurial businesses, speculative real estate ventures, and the more aggressive stocks. They tolerate fluctuations in their assets well, taking losses like boxers who know they will live to fight again.

To their more conservative spouses, the fiscally aggressive are a constant menace, always keeping financial life on the brink of calamity.

The risk affinitive stand to make huge amounts of money. Most millionaires, at some point, gambled big with everything they had. The problem is, so did most former millionaires. Those who err on the side of fiscal aggression can—and very frequently do—lose it all.

Profile of the Risk Aversive

Those who are risk aversive spend their time hunting for that elusive sure thing. Sacrificing high returns for safety at every juncture, they move slowly, cautiously, through their financial lives.

These conservatives perceive money as a pool of assets which, once risked and lost, isn't easily replenished. Self-appointed stewards of that pool, they guard it against danger and invest it gingerly.

They'll tell you, at every opportunity, how hard they worked for that money. Their risk comfort zone is narrow, well defined. Any movement toward the extreme trips an elaborate network of emotional alarms.

Risk aversive investors stash their money in Treasury bills, bonds,* certificates of deposit,** conservative utilities,*** or blue-chip stocks.**** Taking risks in the form of debt, 'creative financing' maneuvers, and even capital investments to start up their own businesses are resisted tenaciously.

To more aggressive partners, the fiscally conservative seem stagnant and plodding. Terrible setbacks are rare; but so are big, adrenalized successes.

The risk aversive err on the side of safety. By sending up a red flag at the sight of anything that looks slightly unsafe, they fail to take risks that are necessary for their own financial well-being. The too timid investor actually squanders money in the form of lost potential income and missed opportunities.

What's Going On

The willingness to risk is inextricably bound to larger issues of trust, confidence, knowledge, and commitment. For David (one of the risk affinitive) and Corine (one of the risk aversive), there was more to their argument than the comparatively simple question: Should they start their own business now or later?

"I guess I really don't trust David to make good on his promise," said Corine, once she calmed down. "I was raised in a real stable home. My dad never invested money in anything he considered 'flaky.' And he considered almost everything flaky.

"I just don't understand how risking the roof over our heads will make our life any better," she continued. "What if David doesn't get all those jobs he says will come to him? And how long will we have to struggle before we make the kind of money we're already making now? He's let me down so many times before."

---

* Bonds – simply an I.O.U. The certificate can be issued by the government or a corporation and describes the terms of the loan.

** Certificate of Deposit – when you place your money in the bank and promise not to take it out for some specific period of time, like 3 or 6 months, or 1 or more years. It pays higher interest than a standard savings account, and charges penalties if you want your money sooner than you agreed.

*** utilities – stock in power-generation companies, telephone or other areas where you would expect to pay your utility bill.

**** Blue Chip Stocks – refers to the large familiar corporations which have been around a long time, such as IBM, General Motors, 3M, and so on.

"Your father gave you some good instructions about money," I ventured. "He also handed down some rigid, opinionated laws that may or may not be appropriate in this situation. For example, do you consider David's work flaky?"

"Of course not," she retorted, clearly offended. "David is really good at what he does. He's the best builder in his company. I know he could do well on his own. It's just that there are so many gambles involved."

"This isn't some fly-by-night idea, Corine," said David. "I've given this a lot of thought. I've sat in the same job for ten years watching guys my own age break out on their own and make fortunes. I just can't keep doing what I'm doing. I don't care what the gambles are."

"I don't think it's actually the new business that's bothering Corine," I began cautiously, turning to David. "It's the level of risk. She's watched so much money disappear since you two have been together. She's also not as psychologically predisposed to risk-taking as you are.

"I happen to think this might be the right time to start your own business. But rocketing into it as you've rocketed into many other deals isn't the way to make it work. Would you both be willing to consider starting the construction business at a lower level of risk?"

They both nodded. It was the first time I had ever seen them agree with each other.

When Risk Is Out of Control... And When It Isn't

There's a significant difference between prudent risk (say, putting money in a well-performing stock) and wild gambles (like investing in a ski resort in the Arctic Circle). Before you put one dime of partnership funds into any investment, know that difference.

In a wild gamble:

- Risk is taken on as a form of entertainment, not founded on methodical financial reasoning.

- You stand to lose large amounts of money—fast.

- You have little or no control over the outcome. (When you play a slot machine, for example, it's up to the machine alone whether you'll win or lose your money.)

In a prudent risk:

- Risk is calculated based on highly probable financial returns, not on ego or how much fun you'll be having. Thrills are sought in other areas of life.

- The investment changes slowly; it's difficult to lose your entire investment quickly.

- Your investments are tailored so you can limit losses. (For example, using a 'stop-loss order'* on stocks gives you a way out of your investment before you lose an unacceptable amount of money.)

There was a vast difference between the nature of risk David would take in starting a new business and the gambles he'd taken in the past. By owning his own company he would be physically and mentally in control of producing results. The venture also had good timing and proper circumstances on its side. The construction business was in a period of growth and he knew the industry well.

At first, Corine saw no difference between this and his other 'goofball schemes.' She'd been burned before. Once the difference between prudent risks and wild gambles was explained, she saw the venture in a new light.

Finding Your Partnership's RAL

Your partnership has a character, behavior pattern, and nuance all its own. As your relationship develops, your mutual Risk Acceptance Level will emerge. Always, always honor that level.

When making any investment or significant financial move, you and your partner should ask yourselves the following questions.

---

* Stop-loss order – You would request this of your stock broker to protect you in case you guessed wrong on the direction that the market would go. As an example, you could say, "If the stock goes as low as 50 (or any price you chose), sell my shares to save me from more losses."

1. What is our financial objective in taking this risk, relative to our mutual goals?

2. How will our present financial needs be impacted?

3. What is the potential return on this investment?

4. What assumptions have we made in determining this potential return?

5. Are the assumptions realistic?

6. What track record is available and how good is it?

7. What could go wrong?

8. Is the potential reward worth the risk to both of us?

9. Are we overcommitting ourselves to this investment at the expense of a balanced portfolio?

10. Can we both live with this investment?

11. If we disagree about this risk, is there a way to offset the risk with greater security in some other area (such as committing more money to low-risk bonds or savings)?

Diversifying Investments and Bringing Peace to the Portfolio

Living with risk sensibly means diversifying your financial portfolio; that is, spreading your money across several unrelated investment categories. The more risky, high-yield investments are cushioned by other, more secure ventures. A well-diversified portfolio contains something for each partner. And you don't need a $100,000 stock portfolio in order to diversify. It can start with two or three small mutual fund investments*after putting your emergency savings in a money market account.

The diversified portfolio satisfies needs for both security and risk. It tempers the too aggressive and too conservative tendencies

---

* mutual funds – a group of stocks, bonds or other securities managed by a professional investment manager or company.

and encourages balanced financial behavior. The level of maximum allowable risk of each partner is never violated.

To diversify portfolios, the best method is called 'asset allocation.' Quite simply, it means dividing your assets or investments so that the overall risk is reduced while the total return is increased. This is, of course, easier said than done and starts with a clear understanding of what risk and total return mean in the investment world.

To make this work for you, consider your age, income level, and financial goals and the relationship of risk to return on each of your investments. Then allocate your assets among several different investment classes: stocks, bonds, precious metals, real estate, international investments, and cash.

I drew two asset allocation models for Corine and David. The first showed the risk curve of their present portfolio; the second reflected a more balanced allocation of assets. The dots on the following chart represent the level of potential risk they are taking as well as the potential return they could expect from each of their investments. They could see clearly from the chart that their investments were not well diversified and exposed them to more risk than they wanted. With a few changes, we were able to balance their investments to accommodate the risk of the new construction business. The limited partnerships were a poor investment to begin with and a sore point for Corinne. They are illiquid, though, so they will continue to hold them even though they have little value.

To devise your own asset allocation model, use the following simple procedures:

Draw two asset allocation models like the ones we created for Corine and David on the next page.

Model # 1

❑ Determine which investments you now have—real estate, CDs, international stock or bond funds, over-the-counter stocks, blue-chip stocks. Your business can even be an investment with a predetermined level of risk. (Entrepreneurial ventures are more volatile than steady employment in a large company, for example.)

ASSET ALLOCATION MODEL
Asset Allocation Model for Corine and David

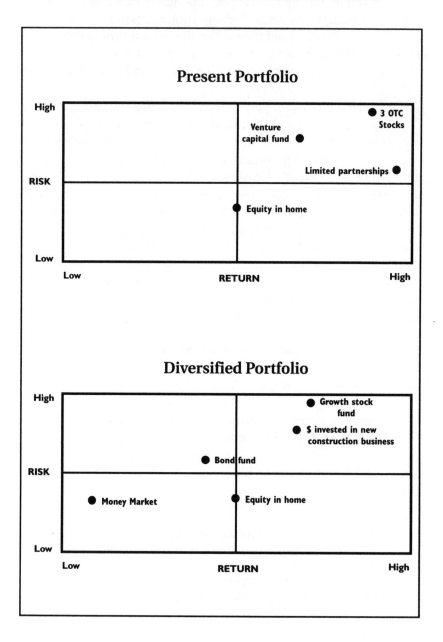

Present Portfolio

High

RISK

Low

Low   RETURN   High

3 OTC Stocks

Venture capital fund ●

Limited partnerships ●

● Equity in home

Diversified Portfolio

High

RISK

Low

Low   RETURN   High

● Growth stock fund

● $ invested in new construction business

● Bond fund

● Money Market

● Equity in home

❑ With the vertical axis indicating the level of return, and the horizontal axis the level of risk, note each investment in its proper quadrant.

❑ Are all your investments clustered into one quadrant? Are they spread out over two or three quadrants? A diversified portfolio has a balanced percentage of assets in two or more quadrants.

❑ You both intuitively know your levels of risk affinity or aversion. With those in mind, look at each investment. What kind of return would satisfy you? What percentage of decline would be intolerable? Is your money working as effectively as it could? Is it in jeopardy?

Model #2

❑ Use the second model to design a more diversified portfolio with the goal of reducing overall risk and at the same time increasing total return. Allocate your investment dollars into several asset classes that have low correlation (that is, little relationship to one another—if the stock market goes down, there will be money in money markets or Treasury bills to cushion the blow). The ideal would be to have all investments in the northeast quadrant—low-risk, high-return. Unfortunately, ideal is different from the real world, so it's best to spread assets so they are not all clumped in any one quadrant.

❑ Depending on your age and objectives, you might want to use the following allocations to reduce risk and improve returns.

To minimize the risk of your more volatile investments, use dollar/cost averaging. That is, invest a set amount of money in a particular stock or mutual fund each month, regardless of whether you feel the market is up or down. Using this strategy over time, you'll find that your average cost per share is less than your average price per share. This is because that same amount of dollars—whether $100 or $10,000—buys more shares when the market is down and fewer shares when the market is up. Overall, studies show that people enjoy a better return using dollar/cost averaging than they do trying to time the market and invest when it's 'hot.' Dollar/cost averaging, then, helps you avoid the most natural tendency investors have—to buy when the market is up and sell when it takes a dive.

Risking Together

"What would help you feel more secure about the risk involved in David's new business?" I asked Corine.

"Well," she said, biting her lip as she considered options she previously never even thought were available. "First, I would have to have some say about what was going on, on a daily basis. Also, I don't want everything we own to be at stake. We could put some money into safer investments."

"Would those actions help you feel differently about his new business?" I asked.

"Yes," she said, "of course."

Together they negotiated a compromise, which they put in writing. David agreed to proceed more slowly, accumulating capital for a year before quitting his present job. That would allow them to leave more equity in their home. Money was taken out of all the high-stake partnerships and all but one of the more volatile stocks. We redirected it into safer bonds and a money market account. They used the dollar/cost averaging strategy for investing in a growth mutual fund.

The initial risks of starting the new business were minimized. Once it began to show profit, of course, the money could be moved back into more aggressive investments.

At Corine's request, they also built into their agreement a 'stop loss mechanism.' After the initial investment, no other money would be used to support the business. It would live or die on its own merits.

Corine was hired as office manager for the project, overseeing the daily inflows and outflows of money. Eventually, she acquired a sense of the financial ebb and flow that businesses always experience. Risks became far less formidable.

Look at your present asset allocation model. Are you and your partner both content with the investments you have? Are you both content with each other's risk behavior? Does one of you feel threatened emotionally or unstable financially? Is there a financial move that might alleviate that threat and instability? Discuss these feelings and thoughts with your partner. Make one move this week to diversify your risks and honor each partner's risk threshold.

Of all the risks you take with money, you don't also have to take risks with your marriage. By merging lives, you also merge finances, and nothing you can do in business can make you more vulnerable than that. As long as you live you will be risking money. The secret is knowing how to take prudent, profitable financial risks while not placing your relationship at stake.

Chapter EIGHT

Tactical Decision-Making and Ending the Paperwork Wars

*Truth #8: If you keep doing what you've
been doing, you'll get more of what
you've got.*

Karen and Charles marched into my office, late for their appointment. Each carried a large box full of what I feared were their financial records. My fears were realized.

While it's usually not my job as a financial planner to nurse clients through the mundane tasks of sorting and filing, their paperwork, Karen and Charles were also my friends. And they needed help—badly.

I sat dumbfounded as they unloaded the contents of the boxes on my desk, making two enormous piles. Sifting then began. The two large heaps were dispersed into smaller stacks of receipts, old checkbook records, past tax returns, and assorted bank overdraft notices.

"Here it is," Charles said. "This is the whole ball of wax. Not a pretty sight, huh? Well—we're here to get organized. Where do we go from here?"

Good News for the Organizationally Impaired

The modern world operates through paperwork—reams upon reams of it. It takes the form of bills, bank statements, records, paychecks, vouchers and receipts.

Each area of personal and business finance creates a paper trail. If you keep yours well manicured and organized, your creditors will love you, the bank will applaud you, your less-gifted friends will wonder how you do it, and the I.R.S. will stay off your back.

If your paper trail is a wild, overgrown, twisted path strewn with errors made, records lost, checks bounced, unreconciled accounts not reconciled and receipts left God knows where, there will be no end to your penance.

Financial planners and accountants tend to see more victims of paperwork wars than lucky victors. Couples fed up with trying to sort it all out, eventually end up turning to professionals.

If you find yourself organizationally impaired, the good news is, you can live a very full life without saving every receipt. It is not possible to reach your goals and live harmoniously in your marriage, however, without some degree of organization. As with every other domain of money life, how well your financial portfolio is organized is determined largely by the nature of your psychological portfolio.

How important is knowing where you stand financially? How important is not knowing? For some, confusion can be a miraculous buffer between personal self-esteem and the hard, bottom-line reality of how much they are quantifiably worth. For others, neatness can be a diversion from the pursuit of other larger goals.

Organization is most commonly a problem in marriages when it's a talent neither partner can claim. Money fights can actually be worse, though, when one partner values the neat and tidy while the other values everything but the neat and tidy. The most heated resentments flare when one partner always has to clean up the other's financial messes.

While few marriages end because of bad bill-paying habits, organization problems can be symptomatic of deeper turmoil. Or they can serve as catalysts, bringing more profound and divisive money differences to a head.

As you remember, the continuum of organization style is banked by two extreme types: Particularists and Generalists. Each has very distinct characteristics. Where would you place you and your partner on this line?

Generalist..Particularist

ORGANIZATIONAL STYLE

Profile of the 'Generalist'

Generalists like Karen and Charles view bookkeeping and accounting as the bane of an otherwise perfect universe. Instead, financial life is understood in only the more general sense: how much comes in/how much goes out. Period.

Ask them specifics and their minds wander to memories of better days in southern hemispheres.

The daily flow of mail and paperwork forms unsightly stacks on dresser tops. Receipts fill the far reaches of purses and pockets. Not only do generalists hate balancing checkbooks, they don't really like to write down checks. Tax time, of course, is a Fellini movie complete with late-night sessions, missing documents, unclear figures, and mounds of papers.

Profile of the 'Particularist'

Particularists live in the domain of detail. Astute and vigilant, they track each dollar as it marches through their household. Records are immaculate. Checkbooks are never even a nickel off. They can tell you how much more they spent last month than this month. Desktops are empty, with a spit-polish shine. Files are neat. Financial life runs with Swisswatch accuracy.

Most particularists will have you believe that generalists are 'wrong' in a cosmic sense. They aren't fulfilling their rightful role as adults. If you've ever been audited by the I.R.S. or had to figure out where an error was on a bank statement under the accusing eye of an unsympathetic teller, you know: Today's institutionalized society was made by and for particularists.

What's Going On?

"I can balance your checkbooks and help get your tax returns filed on time," I told Karen and Charles. "But I'd lay money on the fact that you'll be back, in six months or a year, with your finances in the same condition.

"There's an old saying I like to use in situations like this: 'Give a starving person a fish, and feed him for one meal. Or teach him to fish, and feed him for a lifetime.' Would you two like to learn what you can do about this?"

"We'd be willing to consider it," mused Karen. "What do you have in mind?"

"I have no intention of turning you into accountants, but I would love to see you become better at handling your paperwork. I think you'll have less anxiety and a lot more peace of mind.

"Let's start by looking at what's really going on. Answer me this: How were these chores handled when you were children? What Hidden Investments are at work here?"

"I was raised rich, real rich," Charles said, with a beguiling, boyish grin. "Hell, I didn't even know where our money came from. I surely never saw a bill get paid. Things were just handled somewhere behind the scenes—like magic.

"I brought that early non-training into adult life. I still seem to think someone's going to come along and do it for me. But it won't be Karen. She's worse than I am about it."

We sorted through the records and finally came up with a rough net worth statement. Karen and Charles had few assets, a whopping credit card debt, and their joint income for the year was $98,000. "So what are you gaining by having all this confusion?" I asked pointedly. Clearly, for Karen and Charles, ignorance of the financial facts was paying off in some way.

"I guess by not really knowing how much we had—or didn't have—we could talk ourselves into thinking things were going just fine," said Karen soberly as she looked through the figures.

Confusion to Karen and Charles, as to many people, isn't just a problem. On some level, it's a perceived asset. And procrastination is the means by which confusion works.

The Procrastination Trap

"There's so much to do, no time to do it in, and I don't want to do it anyway. So why start?"

So goes the interior monologue of the procrastinator. If that is a conversation you recognize, you'll want to pay close attention here.

Procrastination kills energy, saps vitality, stagnates creativity, and wreaks havoc financially. It sabotages any real commitment to goals, turning every strategy into vapid dreams and wishful thinking.

Procrastination is also naive. It's a childish assumption that if you just wait things out, they'll get better on their own. Someone might rescue you. Or the problem will simply go away.

There are three methods to the madness of procrastination.

Perfectionism

"When I have more information I'll do it," or "Until I can afford to do it right, I'm not going to do it," or "When my relationship is better I'll do it." These are the promises of the procrastinating perfectionist. Of course, if you waited until conditions were perfect before you started any project, nothing would ever get done. The perfectionist is perennially 'about to begin'—demanding the best and creating the worst.

Excusability

"I don't have the time to do this." "I'm too tired." "You should have done this for me." "We need a secretary to do this." "My hard disk crashed." "The batteries are dead in my calculator." "My astrological chart told me to stay in bed." The procrastinator will drum up a million excuses why he or she can't meet the commitments.

Not only do excuses absolve our procrastination, but procrastination itself makes it possible for us to excuse ourselves. We all know people who put off tasks until the eleventh hour. Then when the job is poorly done, they have a ready-made excuse: "Time was so short, what can you expect?"

Rebellion

"To hell with the I.R.S. If they want my money, they can wait until I'm ready to give it to them." Procrastination is a passive act of aggression. Procrastinating rebels are paying back their partners, parents, banks, God, and any other financial authority for heaping upon them a responsibility they never asked to handle.

If you aren't meeting the most basic due-diligence tasks, you probably aren't sure how organization can help you reach your objectives.

"No one ever got rich from balancing their checkbook," a generalist friend once chided me. While it's true you will not earn your first million by writing down every check, you won't keep your first million without doing it.

There are several techniques I've used to help couples end the paperwork wars and establish financially enriching and emotionally supportive routines.

Do Today What You'd Rather Put Off Till Tomorrow

1. Know your Hidden Investments.

Where do your organizational habits come from? What are you telling each other or the world by not handling the details of your finances? What would it take for you to let go of your old messages about the job being 'boring,' 'too difficult,' or 'too much trouble'?

2. Know the consequences of procrastination in emotional and financial terms.

Only the very lucky avoid serious financial mishaps while avoiding organizing their financial records. Chances are, you aren't one of them. Every bounced check, tax penalty, overdue bill, and every bank mistake you don't catch incurs an expense—in real dollars. Calculate each expense. It will inspire you to modify some very costly habits.

3. Break down the job of organizing your finances into manageable chunks.

Do it as you would eat a pizza—one piece at a time. The task looming in your mind is rarely as insurmountable as what really awaits you. Tackle each of the following arenas separately.

- ✓ Checkbooks and bank statements
- ✓ Tax records
- ✓ Receipts
- ✓ Investment information (prospectuses, brokerage statements)
- ✓ Cash-flow management (CFM systems charts)
- ✓ Bills (to be paid)

Divide and Conquer

Your relationship is one of the best weapons you have to defeat the paperwork enemy. When you enlist each other in sorting out your financial world, you can quell small problems before they become big ones.

1. Redivide tasks between you.

Delegate work to be done based on talents and money styles. Forget about habit ("Oh, but we've always done it this way"); gender ("I'm the man/woman of the house; this is my job"), or any other arbitrary standard. Sharing financial tasks well means knowing where you are each positioned on the organization continuum, and making the most of your differences. For example, particularists are better at such projects as checkbook balancing; they have the patience to track that missing $2. Generalists are good at spotting trends and can be great at investment ideas.

2. Know what you can realistically expect from each other.

If there are tasks you know neither one of you will ever do, hire a professional. Though the initial cost of a financial planner, accountant, bookkeeper, or secretary may be off-putting, what it will save your relationship in terms of worry, stress, blame and argument will be well worth the money.

Check-Ins, Money Dates and Pats on the Back

Not all generalists are organizationally incompetent—just inconsistent. Great flashes of inspiration and flurries of activity are followed by long periods of indolence and avoidance.

The trick to dispatching organization problems is in keeping up with tasks, hour by hour and day by day. Developing the habit of monitoring your money will take practice before it becomes automatic, just as at one time you had to remember to brush your teeth, before it became an unthinking morning ritual.

The best ways I've discovered to ritualize financial organization are:

1. Use the basket system and the 'fifteen-minute check-in.'

All incoming and outgoing paperwork should be put into a basket. For one month, schedule weekly review meetings with your partner. Make them at the same time, in the same place. For fifteen minutes go over the contents of the basket. Review financial transactions, make sure checkbooks are updated, open the mail, file all receipts, and, twice a month, pay bills. Let nothing accumulate.

2. Set up monthly 'money dates.'

Assess your progress in a more general way once a month. Use the time to set goals and assess progress toward them. (We'll be talking more about this later on.) Discuss how effective your spending, saving, and bookkeeping practices have been, and make plans for the next month. When agreements aren't being kept, look at how tasks might be better handled in the future. After the talk, enjoy dinner at a favorite restaurant. Misery and organization don't always have to be bedfellows.

3. Reward each accomplishment.

Astute monitoring always pays off. Whether it's finding a bank statement error in your favor or an uncashed check beneath the sofa pillows, wasted dollars and unnecessary expenditures always come to light. Use some of that 'found' wealth to do something wonderful for yourselves. Make a new investment, or take a weekend vacation.

For decades, psychologists have known that rewards are the key incentive to changing behavior patterns. Yet it's amazing how many couples don't give themselves (and each other) those well-deserved pats on the back. Rewards aren't just a good idea—they're indispensable. Chances are you will never change your habits, once and for all, without them.

"Managing our financial details has made us healthy, wealthy, and wise," joked Charles when I ran into him months later.

"Well, yes—I'm exaggerating. Seriously, though, things are going much better. We hired a bookkeeper to do all the accounting and checkbook balancing, which we both hate. But we keep track of which bills are going out, and how investments are performing, and its really paid off. We were losing money in some stocks we forgot we had. We're also learning a lot more about each other."

Make a list of the areas of your financial life that need organizing. What tasks make you feel anxious? What have you been avoiding? This month, follow the guidelines for overcoming procrastination and getting paperwork done. Notice any changes in the financial landscape or changes in your relationship.

Contrary to what many staunch particularists would have you believe, organization is not an end in itself. It's useful only to the degree that it allows you to soar beyond mundane details, to enjoy the more exciting aspects of life together.

Tactical Decision-Making

Shannon and Jesse

"Don't you think we should go down to the travel agent and pick up those tickets for Jamaica?" Shannon asked as she rifled through her dresser in search of her blue bikini.

"We're not going," replied Jesse tersely, barely looking up from the work he was doing at his desk.

"Oh, God, you're not going to change your mind on me again, are you?" she screamed. "That's the third time this week. What's wrong with you? One minute we're going—the next minute we're not. Yesterday you said we'd work out the money problem somehow. Now today we're broke again. I wouldn't go with you on that vacation now if you handed me those tickets on a silver platter!"

How do you make financial decisions? Do you dive right in? Do you consider every alternative and wade in one slow step at a time? From what I've seen, the simple differences in how couples make decisions and take action can either enhance a love/money marriage or bring it to its knees.

More than a few individuals I know circumvent the problem by making unilateral decisions. As one exasperated woman once told me: "My husband is so damn slow at making up his mind, I just go ahead and do things my way. Otherwise, nothing would ever get accomplished."

It's not a line of thinking I encourage. After all, unilateral decisions are power plays that usually get the perpetrator broadsided by a payback down the line. All decisions do not need to be made together, but agreements about how decisions will be made unquestionably must.

Remember the old '80-20' rule: 80 percent of what you get comes from 20 percent of what you do; 80 percent of the benefit comes from 20 percent of the work.

When it comes to making financial decisions, doing too little (acting in haste with no attention to details) or doing too much (overplanning and overcontemplating) both produce diminishing returns.

There is an optimal time in which all your decisions should be made, a pivotal moment when all facts and feelings converge into a signal to take action.

What happens when that message is different for each partner? Or when the stalling of one spouse enrages the other? Or when the impetuousness of one results in unsound decisions?

On the continuum of decision-making, most people occupy the middle range between extremes of Reflective and Impulsive. Of course, few people are entirely consistent. Some decisions will be cautiously deliberated and others will be made in a flight of whimsy. Take a moment to determine where you and your partner might be on this continuum and then let's look at these extremes.

Impulsive...Reflective

DECISION-MAKING STYLE

Profile of the 'Impulsive'

"You snooze, you lose," the impulsive will caution you. It's better to act and pay the consequences than to wallow in uncertainty and do nothing.

The impulsive anchors onto only the salient features of any financial choice, sailing past all the subclauses and small print. The fewer alternatives offered, the better. Sorting through options is agonizingly dull.

Impulsive decision-makers see and hear what they want to see and hear. They are magnificent examples of selective memory at work. If a business deal 'looks good,' they virtually ignore all evidence to the contrary. They rely on gut feeling, instinct, and seat-of-the pants thinking. Don't bother them with the facts.

In their zealous flight from decision to decision, impulsives get tripped up in their own unreasonable expectations and incomplete assessments. Overlooked specifics of a financial choice come back to haunt them.

The spouses of the truly impulsive polarize into being mistrustful and vigilant. They don't want to be swept up emotionally in the rash, spontaneous drama of it all. If not counterbalanced by some latent reflectiveness, the financially impulsive burn out fast.

Profile of the 'Reflective'

Reflective financial decision-makers weigh all the facts before they put down a dollar. They gather information slowly, shoveling through a ton of information to get the nuggets they need. Every option is considered against all other possible options.

Take them out for ice cream, they'll weigh the relative difference between Mocha Almond Fudge and Cherries Jubilee, Swiss Vanilla Custard or Rocky Road.

Unlike their impulsive cousins, reflectives consider everything, study every angle, and always read the fine print. The problem is, left to their own instincts, they won't stop reading it. They get lost in those details, often unable to make it through the labyrinth of their own mind to take action.

Their inner voices chatter incessantly. "Should I or shouldn't I?" "What if...?"

Reflectives wait for all the facts to be in. And all the facts are never in. Their mates live through a whole range of emotions, from excitement to disgust, as their spouses make up their minds and change them again.

Their indolence is their greatest adversary. The economic and business worlds, and their own mates, march faster than they do. Opportunities pass them by while they postpone, hesitate, delay, debate, and wait for the time to be right.

Decision-Making: What's Going On

Shannon and Jesse found, over the years, that they ran into the same problem again and again. The form changed; the frustration never did. The problem was that their decision-to-action ratio was out of balance.

Lured by the prospect of a vacation (even one they couldn't quite afford) Shannon was ready to charge the tickets and call the taxi—and pay the financial consequences when she got back.

Jesse remained entrenched in the debate between fiscal responsibility and the more exotic pleasures of lying in the sun, daiquiri in hand. The two compelling scenarios alternated in his mind with equal intensity.

The incessant reflecting and reconsidering left Shannon simmering.

The Impulsive and the Reflective may, like Shannon and Jesse, end up making the same financial decision. The two eventually went to Jamaica. Yet, they took action at different speeds, with varying degrees of confidence. Why?

Making or withholding a decision can be a power play—a tactic to control a spouse, employee, or anyone else who must look to you to decide. Quite obviously, the one making the decision holds all the cards.

Decision-making is more than that. It's a reflection of our core beliefs and cognitive processes. Like all the financial behavior we've looked at, financial decisions are a function of the psychological portfolio. What Hidden Investments are present? How has life rewarded or punished the decisions made?

I asked this couple some questions: Have you been badly burned by a decision made in haste? Have you lost out on a big opportunity because you failed to act quickly? What did your parents tell you about your abilities? How much confidence did they instill in you?

"I was raised to be the soul of responsibility," Jesse explained. "I was the oldest child in a large family. My parents left a lot up to me at a very early age. My brothers and sisters depended on the decisions I made. I was pretty young to take on that burden and I remember being terrified of making mistakes. Later on, though, that caution paid off. I can think of a lot of instances in business where holding back saved my skin."

"Have there been times when holding back didn't pay off? When a great opportunity passed you by?"

"Sure. A few of those have gone under the bridge."

"So being extremely reflective doesn't always pay off, does it?"

"No," he said, "not always."

"And what goes through your mind when you make a decision, Shannon?" I asked.

"I don't know about that," she said. "Mostly, I tend to feel if I don't have something right away, I'll never have it. It's a scary feeling, really. It's only been in the last year or so I've even had money to spend. There's an underlying thought that if I don't buy what I want right now, the money will disappear and the opportunity will be gone."

"Decision-making is a complicated business," I said. "Impulsive and reflective types rarely change their spots in midlife. What is really necessary, then, is to have a decision-making protocol—a well-established approach to making money choices. Jesse will always waver back and forth. And you, Shannon, will probably always make instantaneous decisions. There are a few techniques, however, that can lend each of your tendencies some balance."

Decision-Making Skills

Making mutual decisions effectively (read: *in a timely manner*) comes down to following four rules:

1. Know only what you need to know.

You'll never have all the information. In fact, by the time you have all the knowledge you think you need to make the right choice, the environment will have changed. Narrow your knowledge to include only essential information, and know that information thoroughly.

2. Cultivate your intuition and use it.

Gut instinct is crucial for cutting through mental ambivalence. When you have an important financial decision to make, friends will come out of the woodwork to give you good, bad, and contradictory advice. You will be stalled in your own mental polemic if you don't understand how to trust your own instincts.

3. Agree on how mutual decisions will be made.

You probably won't make every decision by first consulting your partner. Some decisions can (and should) be made unilaterally—by mutual agreement. Others must be made together. Work out a strategy. One I've found effective is to make a time line; decide how much time the making of a decision will take. For example, agree to take only one week to determine whether you'll buy the new car you both want. After a week, make the choice and stick to it. This will curb the overimpulsive and commit the overreflective.

4. Don't look back.

Buyer's remorse plagues both the Impulsive ("Why didn't I think before I did that?") and the Reflective ("I knew I should have considered the options more closely"). You will live with millions of decisions during your lifetime. Some you will profit from financially. The others you will learn from.

Moving through your money decisions is like learning how to waltz together—getting the steps and the tempo to work together takes time and patience. If you can learn to respect your partner's information and time-line needs, deciding on even major investments can become more graceful and less painless.

Think of an important money decision you made recently as a couple. How did it feel? Did you agree on the decision, in the same time span? Were you at odds? Now think of another decision ahead on the horizon. Discuss how the tactical decision-making techniques we talked about might help that go more smoothly.

If you keep doing what you've been doing, you'll get more of what you've got. Chances are slim that you and your mate will ever adopt the same organizational and decision-making styles. Nor would you want to. At best, you can temper each other's excesses and turn the differences of your psychological portfolios into financial profit.

Chapter NINE

Love and Money
in the Fast Lane

*Truth #9: To be successful in the fast lane, you
will need to adapt to change, maneuvering
with skill, and keep pace with the markets.*

More than at any other time in history, relationships today must
survive in the eye of a hurricane. From the whims of Wall Street to
making ends meet at the grocery store, from the pressures of holding down a two-career marriage to sorting through the finances of
divorce, life in the modern material world is complicated, pressur-
ized, and uncertain.

Until now we've focused on the internal psychological mecha-
nisms that trigger money conflicts; but there are also overwhelming external stresses you're forced to cope with every day. Many
marriages get swept up in the maelstrom and never quite recover
from the carnage.

There are no fixed guidelines for 'proper' love/money behavior. Romantic and economic relationships are becoming so intricate and complex that what you believed about your life yesterday
often doesn't apply today. In the following pages we'll be taking a

deeper look at that complexity and the many kinds of partnerships it affects.

The Dating Game

Mary Jo and Steve

To hear Mary Jo and Steve tell it, their first date began like one of those syrupy romance novels.

MJ had coaxed Steve into eating at Chez Renee, an upscale Art Nouveau eatery famous for its cuisine, elegance, and prices.

"There she was, positively beaming in this white silk dress," said Steve. "The food was incredible. We had two bottles of Merlot and were feeling no pain at all. There was a lot of chemistry going on."

"Then the check arrives, and all of a sudden there's this really uncomfortable silence," MJ chimed in. "I mean, he had invited me to dinner, but I suggested the restaurant. So I pick up the check and go for my purse. I look across the table at my dashing date, and his face is redder than the wine and he looks like he's about to either pour that glass in my lap or make a quick dash for the door. We split the check. But it was over a month before he called me again."

The Discreet Financial Etiquette of Dating

The financial etiquette of first dates is a prime topic. Theories—about whether men should pay for women, women should pay for men, or any combination of the above—come cheap and plentiful. Yet Hidden Investments speak louder than any rule of protocol—and those ingrained messages, fears, beliefs and biases are hard at work in the midst of candlelight and mood music.

Hidden Investments telegraph unspoken messages about how you really feel and what you really want, especially on those first dates while you're sizing each other up.

- "I want to be taken care of, to know someone is there to provide for me."
- "I can take care of myself. I won't be obligated to anyone."
- "I want you to see me as successful and attractive."
- "I'm capable, a good provider."

- "I want to be sure you can be trusted, that you won't take advantage of me."

Many of those subliminal dialogues, or subtexts, were reeling away as the waiter brought the check over to Mary Jo and Steve's table. Through the seemingly inconsequential act of paying a dinner check they were 'telling' each other about their needs for autonomy, power, and self-esteem.

Mary Jo believed she had every obligation to foot her half of the tab. She had a job, after all. She also later confided, "I wasn't sure about my sexual obligations. When a man wines and dines you, sometimes there's an assumption that you'll be paying your share later. In bed. I don't like to be indebted."

Steve couldn't have seen things more differently.

"That restaurant was way out of my league. I thought I'd stretch a little to impress the gorgeous woman I was with. 'Big spender—big man' and all that. When she went for the check I was, well, embarrassed."

Given the high health liabilities involved, singles today are forced to be unromantically blunt about their sexual arrangements. So, too, the complexities of financial life are forcing couples to deal with money matters frankly and fast.

Imagine saying "I expect to pay my own way tonight," or "Since you have a higher income, let's share expenses proportional to what we make," or "I believe a man should pay a woman's way—how do you feel about that?"

Clients of mine who have laid it on the line to their prospective partners report they feel vulnerable, embarrassed, or overly aggressive.

To communicate honestly about your love/money expectations, needs, and beliefs requires you to overcome the powerful taboos set up to thwart you.

In our appearance-oriented society, courtship rituals emphasize looking good. For men, and increasingly for women, looking good means looking successful. Well groomed. Well heeled.

Those not to the manner born must learn to make appearances belie the financial facts.

It isn't uncommon to pretend you're more prosperous than you are, in order to coax your prospective mate a little closer to true love. Once he or she has fallen for you, the reasoning goes, then your financial circumstances won't matter.

If you've ever been vague about how much money you really earned, left out the unseemly details of your financial woes, or hidden your wealth for fear of being taken advantage of, you aren't alone. Dating couples, as a matter of course, are rarely up-front about their financial circumstances.

From what I've observed, the favorite topics to omit include:

- What you can (and can't) afford
- How much money you really have to spend
- How much of the financial responsibilities for courtship you can shoulder
- What the financial arrangements will be, once courtship spending wanes and the financial reality of living as a couple dawns

The problem with not telling the truth about money on those first forays into romance is that there will always be a morning after. The time eventually rolls around for that distinctly unromantic conversation. "Now, sweetheart, we have to have a little talk about money "

It's little wonder such incorruptible romantics as Romeo and Juliet usually die each other's arms long before they have to start filling out income tax returns and paying electric bills.

Demystifying Courtship Finances

The initial awkwardness in bringing up the subject of the financial arrangements of dating is usually dispelled by relief of knowing you can get on with the more satisfying business of falling in love.

"So who should pay for those expensive first dates?" you might be asking.

Certainly, no one system will work on every date, but there are several arrangements that can be made tactfully at the moment when the piper is to be paid or, better yet, in advance.

- The wealthier partner can pay for everything.

- Partners can trade off expenses.
- Expenses can be split, either in half or in proportion to income.

If you are now dating, or are considering dating, it's important to state clearly for yourself what you believe your financial arrangements should be. Understand where those beliefs come from before you present them to your date.

If the right moment for bringing up the subject of money doesn't present itself, then create the right moment. Introduce the topic in general terms ("So what do you think about the budget deficit?") and work your way down to who will pay for the brie and champagne when you go on the picnic next Sunday. Respect your partner's feeling and beliefs as well as what he or she can afford.

Even the most casual lovers are accepting a certain degree of interdependence, laying down rules for how they will relate to each other forever after. To broach openly the question of the finances of dating is to acknowledge your date's financial integrity. That's an intimacy that can only reward you later should the relationship grow into something more.

Two Careers on One Pillow

Barbara and Leonard

"When we first got married, I was just beginning my junior year in college," Barbara remembered. "Leonard had already been a real estate agent for years. All through that time at Berkeley, and while I was in law school and preparing for the bar exam, he acted as my adviser. I'd been in classrooms my entire adult life. It was nice to have someone around who could show me how the 'real world' worked."

"I really enjoyed her counting on my in that way," reflected Leonard. "I made all of the money to support us, and in spite of the financial stress, the structure of the relationship suited me. I'd watched my father play 'head of the household' for thirty years. Being the breadwinner was familiar."

"During my second year with the firm, things started to change," Barbara said. "It was right around the time I got my second raise. I came home really excited. My salary was equal to Leonard's, and I had done it in only two years.

"I came flying through the door and told him. I couldn't believe his reaction. First he kind of brooded about it. Then he started telling me how I should spend the money. I was stunned.

"I said something like, 'It's my money—don't you think I should have something to say about where it goes? I'd really like to open a separate bank account and do some investing on my own.' He just glowered."

"I didn't glower exactly," interrupted Leonard. "But I do remember saying something that surprised even me: 'And where do I fit into your life? Will I ever be a priority? And when do you plan to have children—between trials?'

"We hadn't talked about having kids," he continued, "except in a very general way. First Barbara had law school to finish, then the bar exam, then the job. During our entire marriage, I rarely saw her in daylight, and she often worked nights and weekends too.

"All at once it occurred to me: my wife was already in her early thirties, with no intention of slowing down professionally. I always assumed I'd have a large family, and that I'd be the head of that family. Now, not only didn't she need me to support her, she didn't need my help at all. I felt completely dispensable. Dreams I'd had all my life evaporated because of her almighty career."

Challenges of the Two-Paycheck Marriage

More than half the households in America are supported by two-career couples like Barbara and Leonard. The stresses they report have been both dramatized and lampooned in television shows and movies.

While couples share their lives in the workplace, it has taken a toll on the quality of the life they share at home. The nuclear family has changed irrevocably, as has its traditional financial arrangements. It will take many more years before the psychology of living in these new relationships is fully understood.

Love and Money in the Fast Lane

Over the course of a two-career partnership such as Leonard and Barbara's, financial arrangements can change many times.

When first married, Barbara was financially dependent on Leonard. During her first year at work, her financial contribution become supplementary. Leonard brought home the principal income, which paid the taxes, the mortgage, and the grocery bill. Her income, still much less than his, provided pin money for movie tickets, clothes, and the rest of life's little extras.

As Barbara moved through the ranks at her law firm, she and Leonard soon found themselves on equal financial ground. However, their emotional balance of power and their Hidden Investments didn't change as quickly as their tax brackets.

The challenge facing such two-career couples crystallizes around the issue of interdependence, or 'me-ness' versus 'we-ness.' Where couples once perceived themselves as a single financial unit, many now see themselves as separate financial entities living under the same domestic roof. While the independent income has been hailed as the supreme power equalizer, it has also brought up questions that those in traditional love/money marriages never before had to face.

- How can I keep my own financial independence, and still work to benefit my partnership?

- If money buys power, doesn't it also buy my spouse the power to leave me?

- If I pool my money in the communal till, will I also surrender my authority over it?

- Do independent incomes have to change our sexual roles? What does it mean to be a husband in an age of financially independent wives? What does it mean to be a wife in these competitive, androgynous times?

- How much money, if any, should we pool? How much, if any, should we withhold for personal use?

- Since we both make our own money, should we still be accountable to each other for how we spend it?

Your Money, My Money, or Our Money?

Couples have devised both strange and brilliant ways to reconcile their Hidden Investments with the economics of the two-career marriage.

Some manage to navigate the sensitive terrain quite well and to structure the disbursement of money according to what feels right for both. Some keep everything separate, and divide expenses right down the middle. Others put both paychecks in one pot, never siphoning any off for personal spending. The middle ground between extremes has a million variations.

Those couples who have a harder time reconciling their beliefs with the reality that both spouses work often enter into collusion. One of the more common is for couples to preserve the power structure and protocol of the traditional provider/nurturer marriage—even when the woman is an equal wage earner.

One woman I knew used to fight tooth and nail to win commissions at work, then would return home and obligingly hand her paychecks over to her husband. He would then determine the amount of her monthly allowance.

The 'Yours, Mine, and Ours' System

The pooling and sharing of incomes is a highly personal matter and must be tailored to circumstances and Hidden Investments.

What is crucial is to devise a system that acknowledges both the individuality and mutuality of relationships. That is important, even if only one spouse works. The best model I've seen is the 'Yours, Mine, and Ours' System. It works like this:

- ❑ Open three checking/savings accounts. A brokerage cash management account such as Charles Schwab's Schwab One account, or Merrill Lynch's CMA account provides a checking account with investment options.

- ❑ The joint 'operating account' pays mutually incurred bills, taxes and expenses. (Refer to the JOINT column of your His/Hers Cash Flow Management System.) This account pays money—either equitably or proportional to income—to the individual accounts belonging to each spouse.

- ❑ Individual accounts cover each partner's personal needs, desires, and whims. (Refer to the HIS and HERS sections of your CFM system.) The money allotted to each should be set aside for each to use as he or she wishes.
- ❑ The investments/money markets in the joint account are for emergency use, vacations, and large purchases; the two remaining accounts are for use by each spouse to direct as needs, desires and habits dictate.
- ❑ Credit cards can also function in this manner: one for each spouse and a third card for joint expenditures.

The 'Yours, Mine, and Ours' System allows partners to be simultaneously independent and interdependent. It can also offset the effects of one partner's bad habits. Check bouncers, generalist bookkeepers, and overspenders have to face the consequences of their own actions since they can't blame spouses for problems in separate accounts.

Traditional Marriages— Untraditional Times

Birgit and Taylor

Men and women continue to adopt traditional love/money relationships in these distinctly untraditional times.

Some choose the traditional format out of a belief that "a women's place is still (or once again) in the home." Others just fall into the pattern as part of the natural course of marriage. To some, the traditional marriage is a logical choice for child-rearing.

"I just feel better raising my own kids," said Birgit, a well-educated and previously successful cosmetics saleswoman, now a full-time mother of three. "Day care is so expensive. It would eat up most of what I would make, and I'd just feel guilty all day."

For those who can afford what has now become the luxury of a single-career household, the husband/provider and wife/nurturer arrangement can work well.

It isn't without its problems, nor has it survived the sexual revolution entirely intact. Said Birgit, "Because I don't make the money, it's easy to fall into a pattern where Taylor makes all the decisions. When we disagree about money, he's in a much stronger position that I am. I don't have the financial leverage to back up my opinions.

"The other side to it is that I have worked in the past. I've lived alone and supported myself. That experience is still with me. For the privilege of raising my own kids, I'm not about to deny my own intelligence and power. We run into a lot of snags with this."

The Energy-Dollar System

Does it matter that one of you is supporting your family with a briefcase while the other does it with a vacuum cleaner? That one of you computes second-quarter earnings while the other computes the relative price of Pampers? Not in the least.

Among modern traditionals, energy spent should mean dollars earned. In an economic unit, all jobs—paid or unpaid—are important.

One rule of thumb that feminists have long touted is to assign a wage for every job the nurturer performs. Compensate her (or, in some cases, him) with money relative to the provider's salary.

To be sure, it's hard to argue with the power of the paycheck.. Nonetheless, the 'Yours, Mine, and Ours' System should not be abandoned because only one person earns the money; nor should power-sharing. Where one spouse's economic disadvantage becomes a decision-making disadvantage, paybacks are inevitable.

When She Earns More

Chandra

"I like being with men who can afford to do the things I like to do," Chandra, a divorced thirty-eight year old account executive once told me. "I married for true love once. And I ended up paying all the bills. Now I go out only with men in my own tax bracket."

Even in the best of circumstances, with the most liberated of partners, when the woman earns more than the man, love/money matters are rarely clear-cut.

In the evolution of the female/provider role, Chandra's story is an increasingly common one.

"At first it was great. My husband wanted to be a literature teacher—something I saw as very noble—and I went into sales. Together we kept the rent paid on a little garden apartment. Things were delightful when our salaries were about equal.

"From the day my business took off and I was making three or four times his income, the relationship went to hell. Sex became a rarity. We began to fight. He began to drink. When he would get good and plastered, he'd say things like, 'How would the platinum card-holder like her hamburger?' It was a mess."

Among the couples for whom this modern relationship hybrid works, it works magnificently. As one male client once told me, "Having my wife earn the money we survive on is a relief. Finally, the pressure is off and I can pursue a career choice that really interests me."

For others, Hidden Investments—in particular those investments in formal gender roles—are obstacles to with which to be reckoned. A wealthier wife can represent a swift kick in the husband's ego. Her femininity might be called into question because of the enormous clout her dollars command. While we've all become used to the idea of female equality, no one was quite ready for female supremacy.

Even when the couple is content with the arrangement, the social pressures on them are overwhelming.

"I would be the one talking business news with the guys at parties," Chandra remembers, barely covering her pain, "and there he'd be, tongue-tied. Of course, I knew he had spent the day analyzing *The Brothers Karamazov*. Those men didn't care about that, though. It was emasculating."

While it's considered fine for a woman to marry a wealthier man, adopt his money, and ascend to his lifestyle, men are rarely granted such permission. A man's success reflects positively on his wife. A women's success often casts shadows on a less well to-do husband.

It's the classic Catch-22. The wealthier the woman becomes, the harder it is for her mate to compete. As her income skyrockets, his self-esteem plummets—and often, so does her respect for him.

In my work with women who have inherited money, I've seen many of them unconsciously (and sometimes quite overtly) sabotage their own financial success to bring their relationship back into balance.

Pioneering the New Relationship

Women today are putting skylights in the glass ceiling and are ascending to higher income levels. Their husbands don't always keep pace. It's up to society to adjust to the new order. There's always pain involved when an accepted way of being is about to change.

If you have the mixed blessing of living in one of these pioneer relationships, you can make the going a little easier.

Communicate honestly. Share your feelings about the female/provider role and how it affects you. Start by completing these sentences:

"I feel inadequate when . . ."

"I feel embarrassed when . . ."

"I feel resentful because . . ."

"I feel powerful when . . ."

"I feel good about our relationship when . . ."

Your relationship is a long-term investment. Sometimes you will be making more than your partner; sometimes your partner will rake in more than you. Not all worthy professions pay the same. The least capable doctors can make tens of thousands more than the most capable teachers. As long as the quality of your contribution feels fair and equal, the quantity of dollars each contributes should not really matter.

Divorces and Blended Families

Allison and Craig

"It's really a shame, but Allison, my new wife, ends up paying my ex-wife's rent," Craig explained. "We don't make all that much—and when we write out that support check every month to my ex, it really burns Allison up. She has to sacrifice for my past life.

"No matter what I do, someone is negatively affected. When I was generous with my kids, Allison got mad. When I spent my extra money to take her on a trip, the kids didn't get to go to camp. There's no way to stretch my money to please everyone."

While Craig felt trapped between his obligation to one woman and his love for another, his new wife felt only resentment for having to surrender their shared income to a woman she wished didn't even exist.

The Ascent of the Blended Family

This year there will be one million divorces in the United States. Slightly less than one in two couples will be filing dissolution papers within a year. The sociological tremor that has been rocking the nuclear family off its foundation is having far-reaching effects on the economics of love.

When the bride and groom tie the knot, the bargain often includes children and ex-spouses. The more the merrier? Guess again. If you are paying alimony to your partner's ex-spouse, or helping to foot the orthodontic bills for his or her children, you're already well aware of how sticky those blended-family financial arrangements can be.

Mixing familial loyalties and jealousy with money is about as safe as tinkering with the detonator on a fully armed nuclear bomb.

Horror stories abound.

When ex-spouses don't pay their obligatory child support, it often falls upon the custodial couple (including the partner who never asked for and never wanted the children) to pay for school fees and designer sneakers.

Second spouses, like Allison, frequently suffer the animosity of their partners' failed first marriages. Much of that anger shows up in financial terms. For example, Craig's ex-wife greeted the news of his impending marriage to Allison by hiring a cut-rate attorney, dragging out the divorce papers to search for loopholes in the support agreement, and suing the newlyweds for $15,000.

Visitation rights are also used as weapons of financial leverage. "If you don't pay your dues, you don't see your kids," the reasoning goes.

Living with Stepfamily Liabilities

When you commit to a partner, you take on his or her liabilities as well as assets.

You invest in a package, not just the features you like. You adjust to your partner's taste in furniture and choice of friends. You allow for his or her mistakes, bad habits, past failures—including the failures of past relationships.

Even under the most congenial and cooperative circumstances, stepfamily finance is a tricky and temperamental beast. It demands that you be the consummate diplomat: flexible enough to address everyone else's needs and honest enough to express your own.

There are some rules to keep all the parties from erupting into a disagreeable melee.

✓ Communicate honestly and openly about financial and emotional obligations. The ex-spouse needs to be reassured that financial obligations will be met. The current spouse needs to know he or she is a priority.

✓ Set limits on those financial obligations: How long will the payments go on? What is the maximum amount the obligated spouse should pay in child or spousal support?

✓ Be certain about what those obligations really are. Do the children really need a new computer? Will a used one do? Is it your obligation to buy it?

✓ Double-check legal documents and agreements; see where you are at risk.

✓ The 'Yours, Mine, and Ours' accounting works brilliantly here. All support payments should come out of the responsible partner's personal account. It's only a formality—of course the present spouse is always affected, but it's a way of saying, "These are my obligations and I'm meeting them with as little burden to you as possible."

Rags to Riches/Riches to Rags

Marta and James

When I think of sudden financial changes causing crisis in a marriage, I think of James and Marta. He was a pleasant, rotund chemistry teacher; she, a feisty blonde with a keen wit and pitbull-style financial instincts.

In the heady days of the bull market, Marta grew to love stock jockeying. She had a natural talent for it, a quick, responsive mind, and within a year she had done very well.

James, more a Hedger, disliked her taste for the high-risk/high-return investment. Watching their portfolio double in value in a year took the wind out of his arguments, however. "Besides," he reasoned, "Marta's a pro."

One day she got a tip from a broker about a company ripe for a takeover. It was a plum she couldn't pass up. To James's dismay, she bought a thousand shares of the stock on margin,* maxing out the amount she could borrow.

"This stock is headed for a hundred and fifty dollars," she reassured James. "What do we have to lose?"

One afternoon, the margin call came. Not only had Marta's latest investment tanked, but the stock market was declining. Having been a bull on steroids, it was finally taking a break.

After that, their underlying difference in risk tolerance, spending and saving patterns, and decision-making styles began to surface constantly. They came to me with relationship-threatening money problems. In looking at the Flexibility Continuum, they could see that their differences in adapting to change were causing the most trouble. Where do you and your partner stand on this continuum? Do you make changes when changes are needed to your portfolio, or do you avoid change and plow on despite new information?

---

* on margin – where the brokerage firm loans the investor money to buy stock, similar to making a downpayment and financing your car; usually limited to 50% of the value of the stock.

Adapt to change..Avoid change

FLEXIBILITY

Handling Windfalls, Crisis and Sudden Changes

A well-known sports star making mega-money from endorse-ments is dropped because of drug charges or worse, murder. A young building developer, just scraping by one day, can be giving Donald Trump a run for his money the next. Today's toast of Holly-wood is tomorrow's failed producer of a failed film. Changes in the financial picture happen in a flash. How well do you cope with them?

Sudden losses of wealth, and even sudden windfalls, can de-liver a fatal blow to relationships already suffering from internal rifts.

Like most of the investors who are young, urban and affluent, James and Marta had come of age financially during the honey-moon years of the stock market. Unlike their parents and grandpar-ents, they were unschooled in big-picture economics—the valleys as well as the peaks.

Losing their money was a blow from which they'll have a hard time recovering.

Conversely, striking it suddenly rich can also be a Trojan horse—an apparent blessing with a thousand curses lurking inside. Witness the many lottery winners who have reported that their lives and marriages fell apart with their sudden stroke of luck.

"We were happier before all the jets, yachts, and mansions," a famous actor said on a daytime interview show, speaking of life with his beauty-queen wife. "When all of a sudden we were in the limelight, things became very distracting. There were all these very fancy people with very expensive habits. Everyone wanted some-thing from us. Suddenly we had a million buddies. For a time, we forgot what was really important."

Living in the Material World ... Together

Getting Clear: Prenuptial and Postnuptial Agreements

In spite of their growing popularity, prenuptial and postnuptial contracts still suffer from a bad reputation. What is quite simply a business agreement between spouses-to-be or spouses has been accused of actually corrupting marriages and precipitating divorces.

Such agreements outline the financial specifics of a marriage. They determine how much will remain separate property and how much will be co-mingled. They outline the assets and liabilities present before the uniting of hearts, minds, and checkbooks, and what will happen to those assets and liabilities should the union end because of death or divorce.

They owe their checkered reputation to their own inherent realism. Prenuptial agreements state outright that divorce is possible, in the same way that wills imply death is inevitable. I doubt they have caused very many divorces—just as wills have seldom hastened anyone's passing.

The problem is that media hype has focused more upon the divorce aspect than on the clarifying effects that written contracts can have while a marriage is still intact.

Love/money contracts, whether formal or informal, create a format for discussing marital finances in a down-to-earth manner rare among most blushing brides and grooms. Anything can be included in it, from who pays the health insurance to how the children's schooling will be handled.

Since marriage means not only falling in love but also joining in business, why not get the terms of that business arrangement in black-and-white? I can think of nothing more effective in averting love/money conflicts down the line than a good, clearly written contract. If the legal aspects of these agreements make you squeamish, and you don't want to go through a lawyer, pencil an informal one between yourselves. Going over potential pitfalls in advance can only make you better prepared if and when you actually come upon them.

Coping With Investor Overload

Consider these diverse, but interrelated facts:

- What happened in the stock market yesterday affects the earnings of your pension plan this morning.

- Stock indices rise and fall at giddy speeds. Paper fortunes are made and lost faster than ever.

- Corporate jobs are becoming more precarious; mergers and takeovers, the norm. Industries booming one year can be obsolete the next.

- The new tax laws have instituted more change in the tax structure in the last few years than this nation has known in the last fifty.

- We are now in a global marketplace. What happens from Hong Kong to London affects your investments.

- There are more mutual funds now than there are stocks traded on the New York Stock Exchange.

Every time you turn around, the amount of information you need to know in order to get ahead seems to double. The moment you adjust to the risks of a given financial game, something happens to up the ante. The information overload is nearly unbearable. Just surf the net if you need to be convinced.

I want you to realize that the stresses your relationship is coping with now are unique in history. If the pressure of merely functioning financially is more than you tolerate emotionally, you are not inept—or alone. You didn't miss some all-important day in school when everyone else learned the tax code and how to decipher the hieroglyphics of the financial pages.

Money-related stress is nothing to be taken lightly. Upswings in domestic violence, stress-related illness, and sometimes suicide accompany sudden or dramatic changes in a person's economic picture.

Finding Method in the Madness

Creative Problem-Solving

Handling finances in today's fast lane means dealing with crises as they come at you, like a fighter averting an onslaught of right hooks.

Today's effective money managers are crisis managers, good problem-solvers who can see a critical path through the thicket while others stumble about in the shrubbery. The path consists of five steps:

Define the problem. Begin by listing your major sources of money stress. They may include bookkeeping, losing a job and trying to live on one income, or the financial consequences of a new baby. Get them all on paper clearly. Many times, obvious solutions are overlooked because the problem isn't well stated.

Brainstorm. Start brainstorming—any and every solution you can think of, no matter how absurd or impractical. The most brilliant ideas arrive when the logical side of the brain is given a breather and the creative, uninhabited side is allowed a good romp.

Do a cost/benefit analysis. What would each activity cost you, compared to how much of the problem it would solve?

Go for one solution. Inevitably, one solution will appear better than the others. It will stand out and resonate with some quality of potential or truth. Choose it and implement it.

Monitor and modify. During the following weeks or months, monitor yourselves every two weeks. How are those solutions working? If everything is going well, cut back to quarterly and annual monitoring. Much of money management involves simple upkeep and tending.

When Enough is Enough

Today, the 'good life' is a self-elongating stairway to heaven. One never, in fact, arrives. In a consumer society where the sky's the limit, we find ourselves having to invent new versions of the same products every year, just to keep our economy on its feet.

When we can't pay for the lifestyle, we borrow, borrow, borrow. Domestic debt is high and rising even as you read this.

It is Madison Avenue's divine purpose to get you to want what you don't need. The struggle to pay for it is putting an inordinate pressure on us all.

When I see clients trapped in the game, I sometimes ask: Do you really need, or want, the possessions for which you're striving? When will enough be enough? When will you know you've reached your material goals?

In order to live in the material world happily, you will have to narrow it, define its boundaries, and state what your participation in it will be.

Look over this chapter. Of the many new relationship forms we've looked at, which ones apply to you? Ask yourself, and your mate, whether these suggestions for dealing with those stresses might be helpful. This week, institute one change in your financial or psychological portfolio to make it more adaptive and relevant to your life in the fast lane.

Successful relationships keep pace with the market, keep peace on the home front, and keep money in perspective. To live happily together, you and your mate must become masters of change and fast thinking. You must also know when it's time to draw the shades and settle in quietly with your partner—and ignore the material world pounding at the door.

Chapter TEN

Achieving Financial Independence: Managing Money by Objective, Not by Accident

*Truth #10: When you use a map, you're more
likely to avoid detours and wrong turns.*

Creating a relationship in which love and money work together
is like creating a work of art. As in painting, there are two approaches.

The artist Jackson Pollock was famous for throwing paint at
random onto a huge canvas, then cutting out portions that 'fit' his
vision. Through the 'accident' of his helter-skelter artistic process,
he managed to create abstract masterpieces.

By contrast, Georges Seurat took months, even years, to finish a
single painting. Every speck of color was minutely planned in its re-

lationship to every other speck, and to the picture as a whole. Seurat was the quintessence of painting by objective.

When lovers manage their finances Pollock-style, by 'accident,' they rarely end up with masterpieces. Accident managers more commonly create money relationships in which their hidden investments cause chaos, misunderstanding, and money fights. Their financial life is in disarray. Differences in spending/saving habits and risk thresholds keep partners teetering on the brink of calamity, and life together proceeds from crisis to crisis, bill to bill, never arriving at that point where love and money harmoniously converge.

Couples who manage their financial lives by objective-Seurat-style, with every element serving to enhance the efficiency and beauty of the larger picture, create love/money marriages that are masterpieces in progress.

During my years as a financial planner, I have met many couples who enjoy such positive and powerful relationships. They come from different backgrounds and harbor diverse beliefs. Some are rich, others live modestly. Some are young newlyweds; others, grandparents.

Most had to work hard to get where they are. Reconciling the complexities of both financial and psychological portfolios into a single, congruent approach to life is rarely easy. Having a map or plan to where they wanted to go financially helped them avoid detours and wrong turns.

In the pages that follow you'll meet three of these couples whose relationships exemplify, to me, masterpieces of partnership. What they have to say about money, and the methods they've used to overcome their differences, never cease to inspire me. I hope that the sketches of their relationships recorded here will also inspire you.

Nancy and Paul

When I first met Nancy and Paul, their financial portfolio was far from ideal. They were paying off a load of debts and were living frugally on Nancy's income. The few assets they had were illiquid. Paul was still in medical school, making no money.

What they did have, however, was an exuberant, highly focused approach to dealing with their financial circumstances.

"On our last anniversary we made the commitment to work through our money situation," remembered Paul. "We felt if we could handle that, we could handle anything. We saw it as a vehicle for getting through our major differences."

On Hidden Investments

Said Paul of his early money memories, "My parents never talked about their money. I did notice, though, that my mother drove a Chevy and my father drove a Jaguar XJ6. What I got were two different value systems. One, 'It's possible to live on nothing.' And two, 'Get the very best you can for your money.' I operate somewhere between the Chevy and the Jaguar."

My dad found himself broke on more than one occasion, episodes that sent him tumbling into deep depression. When money was available, he spent it immediately.

"For men, money and sex are tied in together," Paul mused. "Having money, like being a good lover, is a source of status. Your peers think better of you if you're a good provider.

"Relying on Nancy to make all the money while I'm in school hasn't been easy. My ego has suffered. I've had to keep telling myself that men whose wives support them aren't weak or worthless. I'll be solvent again soon. Fortunately, Nancy is very compassionate. She gives me back my perspective when I lose it."

Nancy was raised with similarly diverse money attitudes. "My mother taught me there will always be enough. My father, the main provider, worried a lot about money. He did teach me positive socialistic values: 'Give according to ability. Take according to need.' However, I have to watch out not to fall into the 'have/have not' roles my parents portrayed."

On Communication

When conflicts arose, Nancy and Paul had precise ways to communicate.

Said Nancy, "First I try to cool out, to get clear on what's bugging me. Usually it's not just the money, but fear of being sabotaged or having my power taken away. I get back in touch with my 'source of supply'—which is in me, not my spouse. Then I work with him on things we can do—our checkbook, investments, or whatever—that will change how I'm feeling."

"My tendency is to withdraw," admitted Paul. "We made this standing date every Friday evening to end the week by telling each other what's been going on for us. That includes money. It forces me to communicate about issues I might otherwise keep to myself. If the discussion looks like it's going to turn into a major debate, we make a separate date to talk about it."

On Working Out Differences

"I use money for experiences, for making life better," Nancy explained. "Paul uses it to buy things. This is something I just don't understand. We're good for each other, though. He'll push to get things I'm too practical to buy but really enjoy having. After our initial blowups around this, we began to see how our differences could expand each other's horizons."

"What turned me around was having a relationship with an amazing saver," Paul enthused. "On a teacher's salary she saved enough in four years to make a down payment on a home. In the year after I met her, I paid off loans totaling one third of my gross income.

"We also see the process of making money differently," he continued. "To me, there's never enough to be free of obligations—I see money that way especially when I'm feeling desperate or when I really want to buy something. Nancy is convinced that with proper planning, there will be enough money and everything else. She's really helped me to relax."

On Love/Money Management

Paul and Nancy have always had their shared vision clearly in focus. They knew precisely the direction their love/money relationship would go. To that end they created an 'agreement book,' outlining what needs to be done to reach objectives, who will do what, and by when.

"We don't operate on assumptions," said Nancy. "We write it all down. Occasionally we'll pass the pen back and forth, clarifying and making amendments. It really enhances our sense of fair play."

Anne and Stewart

Anne and Stewart came to me after twenty years of marriage. At that time they were in the stage when most couples, as the writer Joan Didion once said, have "reached the traditional truce, the point at which so many resign themselves to cutting both their losses and their hopes."

Anne and Stewart were not like most couples who arrive at midlife together, though. They had cut neither losses nor hopes. Instead, they remained in the thick of planning and negotiating their lives together.

Early on, they chose a traditional love/money format. Stewart, a vice president for a large marketing consortium, was the sole wage earner. Anne worked in volunteer jobs while her children were small, then gradually schooled herself in finance and took over much of the couple's investing tasks.

They came through their changes in their money status the hard way, through trial and error. They emerged in the end as content suburbanites, financially and emotionally at ease.

On Hidden Investments

"Debt to me is horrifying," said Anne. "Of all the financial challenges we've had to face together, owing money has caused the most problems. My parents lived through the Depression, so I was reared in an ethic of paying cash for everything. Stewart had to nurse me along every time we had to borrow money. He was very kind and reassuring about it, thank God."

"I always respected Anne's fears about debt," said Stewart, "even though borrowing money was sometimes our only option. So I always presented her with the full package, not only how much we'd be borrowing, but when and how it would be paid back."

On Power and Identity

"Anne and I were both raised to be very self-sufficient with money, and that has helped to make us individually strong," Stewart reflected. "When we had our first child we made clear choices about our relationship. I would work and she would stay home and take care of the family. But never did I think she would be subservient to me, or less powerful. It was important to both of us that she have her own identity. If something happened to me, I know Anne would be able to handle the family's finances on her own."

"Some couples just fall into their financial positions, and if they end up happy with their lot in life, they're lucky," added Anne. "We were always goal-oriented and pragmatic. We knew that the best way to reach those personal and financial goals was for Stewart to work at his company and for me to work at home."

On Money Management

The couple did have differences in money styles to adjust to—and that adjustment took years.

"Bookkeeping is a chore for me, right up there with doing windows," said Anne. "At first I did the paperwork because Stewart worked such long hours. Once, as a birthday present, he said he'd do the books for one year. That was twelve years ago and I never took the job back. We do talk constantly about our money status, however. I can tell the communication is slipping when we start blaming each other for money problems. Marriages get into trouble when one partner has no concept of where the money is going."

"I actually like playing with the numbers and doing the paperwork," conceded Stewart. "We've always had separate checking accounts, just to keep things clear. I write her a check at the beginning of the month, and then I never ask her about the money again. It seems to work well; she has her autonomy, and because I trust her and we've made all our agreements in advance, I never worry about where that money is going."

On Changes in the Financial Picture

"I've worked at the same company for many years," said Stewart. "I've made a lot of money, and by most standards, I'm now pretty rich. I watched how my colleagues handled the changes in their financial status. Once they reached their goals, many didn't know what to do with themselves. Some started spending like crazy. Others drank, and a few couples got divorced. Getting rich is a lot like having kids—you're never totally prepared for it. I'm glad I've had Anne around, she is a pillar of common sense."

"We made the decision to hold back," added Anne. "Sure, we traveled and had a nice home. But we were never as extravagant as we could have been. We knew it would be a big mistake to get swept up in a spending frenzy."

On Priorities

To Anne, priorities have always been clear cut. "Our relationship has always been our number-one priority. We always put making money into perspective. If a conflict came up, the needs of the family were first."

"Fortunately, we tend to agree on most major decisions," Stewart added. "When our priorities do differ we give each other a lot of leeway and freedom. When she buys a car, she chooses it. When I buy something for myself, it's my decision. When we really disagree, one of us will give in. The next time, it's the other partner's turn. We find a balance."

On Money Fights

"I think money can be a wonderful place to dump the frustrations from other parts of the relationship," said Anne. "We don't have money conflicts because we don't have other conflicts. You either live in upheaval or you learn to live gracefully beside each other."

Janette and Don

When I first met Don and Janette, they appeared to be model seniors, still affectionate with each other after thirty-five years of marriage and financially ready for the 'golden years' that were headed their way. They had come to me for retirement advice. It didn't take long, though, to realize all was not as it seemed.

"I'm worried about Don," Janette once half-whispered to me on the phone. "He's still under a lot of stress at work—the company is fighting a hostile takeover. He's overweight, and his doctor has already warned him about his health. He has no time to talk about our personal financial situation and won't even discuss making out a will let alone a trust which I think we need. These are supposed to be the best years of our lives. I want to get more involved in managing our money so they turn out that way."

During the year I worked with them, Don and Janette made major changes in their relationship, changes that drove one point home to me: You are never too old, or too set in your ways, to create a new and better love/money partnership.

On Hidden Investments

"I was raised to be a cute little Southern belle," said Janette in her earthy Georgia twang. "Whenever I would mention the subject of money, my father would say, 'Don't worry your pretty little head about it.' I never did learn math, so the sum total of my knowledge about money was how to write a check. Things didn't change much when I married Don. He picked up where my father left off, and we never discussed finances."

"Don't forget," Don interjected, "in those days money talk was considered unseemly and impolite. You'd never tell someone how much you paid for your house, any more than you'd tell them your uncle was a drunk.

"I was raised to protect and take care of women. I dominated our marriage, especially when it came to money, because I considered it my duty."

On Decision Making

Catalysts for change come in many forms. For Don and Janette the transformation began with the arrival of a large sum of money. Janette remembered it well.

"Not too long ago Don's company gave him a bonus of fifty thousand dollars. He was so busy, he just dumped it into a savings account. It bothered me to no end that the money was just sitting there earning hardly any interest. Don was always too busy to discuss it with me.

"I started reading up on investments. I'd clip articles from *Money* magazine and leave them on his night stand and keep the financial news on during dinner. He just wasn't interested in what he considered petty domestic money decisions. Isn't that enough to fry you? And since he had no will, I began to think I'd end up a bag lady if anything happened to my husband. I decided to take matters in my own hands."

"I was the typical preoccupied executive," confessed Don, "and I didn't realize it was upsetting Janette so much. I guess in the back of my mind I never figured she was competent enough to know about money. I didn't give her much credit. I just figured I'd get around to the investing eventually. The whole business of doing estate planning was distasteful.

"After she brought it up enough times, I began to realize how upset she was about all this. I knew if I wanted to keep my marriage, I'd have to wise up and start listening to her."

On Communication

Janette realized that to get Don's attention she'd have to be inventive. "Whenever I brought up the subject of money, I sounded exactly like a nagging, henpecking wife. I realized I was never going to get through to Don if I kept that up. So, I made a plan.

"One Sunday morning while he was relaxing with a cup of coffee, I asked for ten minutes of his time for a little presentation. I brought out a flip chart. On the first page, I'd outlined the problems I saw in the areas of investments and estate planning. On the second page, I outlined the consequences—how much income we were losing each month by having fifty thousand dollars in a savings account. I also described how much probate would cost if he died without a will or trust, and outlined an idea of estate taxes, though I couldn't calculate it exactly. On the third page, I listed solutions.

"I made a point of sounding completely unemotional and businesslike—to really speak his language. There's something about a flip chart and dry presentation that makes a businessman feel right at home."

"It was terrific," agreed Don. "In ten minutes I got the whole picture. I understood why she was so upset all those months. I was even impressed by the solutions she came up with. We went to the estate planner the next day to write a will and create a living trust. During the next month or two, we also put money into some of the investments she suggested. From that time on I've appreciated her in a new way."

On Changing Roles

Don and Janette were typical of transitional couples who have watched male/female financial roles undergo cataclysmic change. They knew they'd have to change also, or become victims of the new financial order.

"When I realized how little I knew about money, I started attending lots of seminars. I got religion fast. I've become a lot more assertive. I'm no longer the cute little lady who wouldn't wrinkle her brow over money matters.

"I even took control of the books, something Don had a real hard time letting go of. Believe me, it wasn't easy. I floundered at first. Eventually, I got the hang of it."

Don's attitude toward his position in the family also underwent a drastic change. "We're now both actively involved in getting where we want to go. We want to retire comfortably and take those trips to Europe we've been depriving ourselves of all these years.

"And I've been a lot less domineering since all this happened. I'm actually happier. I'm spending more time with my kids and Janette—good, intimate time—and I actually enjoy them more since I quit trying to run their lives. As I'm closing in on retirement, I'm starting to understand what Janette has liked about being home all these years."

What Makes Money Relationships Tick?

Most marriages are equal parts joy and struggle. What separates financial relationships that work from those that don't is the degree to which the partners have developed their inner resources.

In truly rich relationships, partners understand their Hidden Investments and maintain constant rapport between internal psychological states and external money choices. They choose their financial roles based on money styles and talents, rather than gender and habit. They keep power moving dynamically between them, neither hoarding nor surrendering it. They communicate fairly and stay focused, adjusting conversations to suit personalities and circumstances. They understand and work with their differences.

Rich relationships are hardy and adaptive to change. They embrace deadlines, crisis, and chaos. They accommodate emotional changes and expand to include new dreams, goals and whims.

Couples who prevail over their financial conflicts know intuitively how to be interdependent, to live full and complete lives as individuals while always remaining linked in partnership. They know that nothing illustrates romantic commitment more graphically than the co-mingling of dollars, and they invest their resources with clarity and trust.

From Management by Accident to Management by Objective

Most important, the best love/money partnerships are in command of their circumstances. Partners know where they are headed and how they will get there. They manage by objective, with the imagination to look toward the best that life can be—and the good sense to know what objectives are obtainable.

By understanding your past and mapping your future together, you, too, can have such a relationship.

Mapping the Future

I find it easiest to approach objectives in tiers, from the ones you dream about in the distant future to the objectives you can obtain tomorrow. Objectives can be more precisely categorized into what you want to

✓ Be (your state of being: to be famous, secure, independent)

✓ Experience (your activities: adventuring, writing, working at a new job)

✓ Accumulate (your possessions: home, car, recreational 'toys,' clothes)

Take a few moments to complete the sentences in the following exercise with your partner.

Ultimate Objectives

Ultimate objectives comprise your personal Utopian dream, the best of all possible worlds for you. When imagining that perfect state, don't be modest or practical. Be outrageous. Lose yourself in life's numberless possibilities.

In the financial relationship of our wildest dreams we would

✓ Be. . .

✓ Experience. . .

✓ Accumulate. . .

Short-Range Objectives

Short-range objectives are destinations you are committed to reaching in the next year—beginning now. They are achievable dreams, reached with reasonable effort.

One year from today, in our financial relationship we will

✓ Be. . .

✓ Experience. . .

✓ Accumulate. . .

Long-Range Objectives

Long-range objectives are the destinations you are committed to arriving at in the next five to ten years. They comprise your long-range projects in progress, slow-maturing investments, and fore-seeable, reachable dreams.

Ten years from today, in our financial relationship we will

✓ Be. . .

✓ Experience. . .

✓ Accumulate. . .

Balancing Portfolios and Taking Action

Rich love/money relationships reconcile the financial and psy-chological portfolios of each partner, bringing them into the single focus of the partnership.

To do this, take a long look at your psychological portfolio (as discussed in Part I) and the different behaviors reflected in your fi-nancial portfolio (Part II). Using the following model, fill in the assets and liabilities of both portfolios, as well as the objectives (both long and short range) you would like those portfolios to build toward.

What you will have is your own 'management by objective' road map: an at-a-glance profile of where you are, where you're going, and what you're willing to do to get yourself there.

William Donoghue, the investment authority and writer, said it best. "The purpose of financial planning is to improve the quality of your life—and to live and love better. Every time I have managed to improve one area, the other improved."

Financial Portfolio

Assets
1. (home, car, stocks)
2.
3.
4.
5.

Liabilities
1. (credit card, debt, mortgage)
2.
3.
4.
5.

Objectives
1. (retire in 6 yrs./$6,000 per month)
2.
3.
4.
5.

Psychological Portfolio

Assets
1. (good communication)
2.
3.
4.
5.

Liabilities
1. (overspending, paperwork)
2.
3.
4.
5.

Actions to be taken
1. (curb spending)
2.
3.
4.
5.

A Word about Action

In my opinion, few things are more powerful than a clearly defined and worthy objective. It exerts a gravitational pull, irresistibly drawing you toward it.

The road between where you are now and your objective isn't a linear trajectory between point A and point B. When you take action and move beyond previous limitations to reach for something more than you now have, unexpected windfalls will happen, simply out of momentum.

In other words, if you're standing at point A, and move toward point B, you may very well find C, D, and E along the way. It's a phenomenon that the scientist/philosopher Buckminster Fuller called the Precessional Effect.

The Precessional Effect can show up in simple or dramatic ways. In the course of cleaning out your files you may find an uncashed check. Or by designing your Cash Flow Management System, you may discover a large, unnecessary expense. Or in working to meet a financial objective at work, you discover a new niche for your talents.

Properly directed motion toward a worthy goal rarely goes unrewarded.

Personal Action Plan

If we are to put all the steps of this book into practice, we might draft a list of actions we are committed to. Use this list as a guideline, personalizing it to who you are as an individual and in relationship. Use this in happiness and prosperity.

✓ We will communicate our opinions and concerns by staying focused and by not blaming each other.

✓ We will gain control over how we use our money.

✓ We will honor each other's differences and hold them as potential sources of strength.

✓ We will understand and communicate our Hidden Investments.

✓ We will tell the truth without backing down or placating.

✓ We will hold love as the framework for our relationship—of which all money decisions are only a part.

Chapter ELEVEN

Financial Fitness for the Next Decade

As we approach the year 2000, we know that managing our personal and financial lives in this fast-paced world is easier in some ways, yet more difficult in others. While the advances in computer technology allow us to track and manage money more quickly and accurately than before, the information overload we experience from brokers, financial advisers, publications and the Internet can create indecision and inaction. Many couples come into my office with a good sense of their values and communicate well about money, yet have concerns about specific issues, such as saving for retirement or funding college for their children. They've tamed the paperwork tiger and have a financial plan for saving and investing, yet that still isn't quite enough. They want to know how to deal with the uncertainty that we're facing as we move forward to the next century.

The eighties were high-flying times when it was easy to make good money almost by accident. By being in the right place at the right time, whether it was real estate or the stock market, our assets grew in value almost magically. Debt was not a four-letter word; it was spelled 'leverage' and seemed to be a powerful way to make even more money. Now we are paying for the overwhelming debt we incurred on both personal and national levels.

As the nineties began, we experienced a tremendous sense of insecurity about our financial institutions—from brokerage houses to S&L's,* from banks to isurance companies. Insecurity surfaced in other ways, too. Our personal lives were affected dramatically as companies were downsized, acquired, or sold.

Frankly, what we learned to trust in the last decade seems less secure than ever before. It's tempting for many now to trust nothing and to do the same.

The mid to late nineties brought new highs in the stock market and new hope for those of the Baby Boom generation, who were finally getting serious about planning for their retirement. When something is so good for so long, we anticipate a correction so strongly that it can become a self-fulfilling prophecy.

As we face the next decade, I don't know whether interest rates or inflation** will be up or down, or just what the stock market will do.

What I do know, though, is that it is time now to do two things:

1. *Reduce the financial stress that affects our personal lives and relationships.*

2. *Design an action plan for managing finances and investments in these changing and uncertain times.*

Here are Some Specific Strategies to Reduce the Financial Stress in Your Life

Share Tasks and Responsibilities

Take a close look right now at who balances the checkbook, does the taxes, investigates investments, makes the financial decisions. Are you satisfied? Is there a better way? The key here is that women—and men—can no longer afford to let the 'other' handle it all.

---

* S&L – Savings & Loan institution.

** inflation – the concept which says the price of goods and services will cost more in the future than they do today. Does *not* apply to all consumer products. Usually expressed as a percentage per year increase.

Both of you must know how to deal with banks, credit cards, insurance, and investments (if you have them). *Both* of you must have the skills, training, and experience to deal with the complex financial world in which we live.

You and your partner should review your financial tasks and obligations. Define or redefine who will do what. Take note of any areas you do not understand or about which you do not feel comfortable. Then sign up for a class, or talk to your accountant, financial planner, or banker. Surf the net or read *Money Magazine*, *Barron's*, the *Wall Street Journal*, or any of the other excellent sources of financial information.

Trade financial tasks with your partner periodically—maybe you'll balance the checkbook for six months, then your partner will. Scary perhaps, but you will both have a better sense of where the money goes. You will also know what to do if the other person is not around to handle things.

Don't wait for an emergency

Your partnership can only be strengthened when both of you are fully capable of managing your financial affairs.

Plan for 'What If's'

The only constant in our lives is change.

What will you do if you or your partner loses a job? Suppose one of you becomes disabled? How will you cope if your company is taken over—or moves elsewhere?

Do contingency planning for any of these unexpected situations. Answer those 'what if' questions with specific 'if then' plans. The old adage about an emergency fund of three months fixed expenses in a money market or other 'liquid' holding* might be a great idea. In practice, though, I find that most people opt for a portfolio of mutual funds, stocks or bonds, so they can earn a bit more but still be liquid. Remember, 'liquid' refers to your ability to gain quick access to your assets in the form of cash. Be sure you and

---

* Liquid holding – cash, or assets which can easily and quickly be converted to cash. Opposite: Real Estate, antiques or art objects.

your partner know what financial resources are available if one of you is disabled, loses a job, or dies.

Invest Your Wealth in Health

The cost of health care in the U. S. shows no sign of decreasing. In fact, the price you pay for good health will probably continue to rise. You and your partner need to investigate your medical coverage and understand how it works.

Unfortunately, an unexpected illness can mean financial disaster. It is estimated that half of all personal bankruptcies are due to health-care costs.

Besides securing good health-care coverage, you are probably also investing time and money in taking good care of yourself. Preventing problems may be the least expensive way to cut your health-care bills.

Inherit Money, Not Problems

In the decade of the 1990s, the 'baby boom' generation inherits eight billion dollars.

Don't pop the champagne yet! Whether you belong to that generation or not, you and your partner need to discuss how you will handle the transfer of family money. The legal reality is that those inheritances and gifts are the separate property of the one who receives them. The financial reality is that those dollars may be needed to ease family finances, purchase a new home or car, or take that dream vacation—all of which benefit you both. Who will have the 'say' about how those funds are saved or spent? What will you do if jealousy, resentment, or a shift in the balance of power threatens your relationship? Don't forget that any strains in the relationship with your parents (or other relatives) can also show up as a problem between you and your partner.

If you have small children of your own when you inherit money, you will have to face another sticky question: How will you protect your interests and those of your children without alienating your partner?

These issues require delicacy and honesty . . . and professional help if you need it. Consult with an estate planning expert in a trusted legal, banking, or financial planning firm.

As with anything else—inherited money does not have to threaten your relationship if you are up-front in dealing with it.

Smooth Out Your Blended Family

Chances are, you and your partner are part of a blended family, complete with ex-spouses, stepchildren and/or extra in-laws.

These multifaceted family ties make it even more important that you establish precise financial agreements among everyone concerned, and get it in writing.

Will you have to contribute alimony to his ex-wife or her ex-husband? Are you both having to pay off the credit cards or bad debts of a former spouse? Who is responsible to which children for what?

As with inherited money, you will have to use a delicate touch to smooth out the rough spots for your stepfamily to truly become blended.

Get Ready for the Triple Squeeze

Are you helping children through college or to buy that first home, paying for Mom and Dad's living expenses, *and* trying to save for your own retirement—all at the same time? If so, welcome to the Triple Squeeze. For women my age the fact is, we'll spend approximately seventeen years caring for our children and eighteen years caring for our parents. This means financially—and emotionally.

The bad news is that this phenomenon is here to stay and will get worse with the aging of America. The good news is that you can lessen the burden by being realistic, setting boundaries, and being honest with others about what you can and cannot do—both financially and emotionally.

Say "No" to Blame

Don't let frustrations and uncertainties about finance turn into blame. Chances are your partner feels just as confused and concerned about money as you do, despite what he or she says. Keep focused on the problem at hand. Suppose you have a bounced check and an argument erupts, ask yourself: *Is this about money, or is this about something else?* If it is the latter, talk it out now or get the professional help you need to discuss your concerns honestly and openly with your partner.

Strategies for Managing Your Finances and Investments in Uncertain Times

Hold a Financial 'Summit' Meeting

To get where you want to go, you must first determine where you are. Update your two most important financial statements—your balance sheet (what you own and what you owe) and your cash flow statement (what comes in and what goes out). Identify how expenses and incomes will be shared.

Set Measurable Goals

Make your financial goals realistic, measurable, and achievable. Break them into manageable 'amount per month' or 'amount per year' steps. If your five year old is going to college in twelve years, how much do you need to put aside monthly and yearly to meet those expenses (given an estimated rate of inflation and rate of return on your investments)?

Schedule Update Meetings

Meet with your partner or spouse to discuss finances on a monthly or weekly basis. In busy lives, it's easy to procrastinate. Having regular financial meetings can help you head problems off before they develop, and will ultimately save you time, money and frustration.

Evaluate Your Current Portfolio

For your investments, know specifically how much you should have in stocks, bonds, and cash to be consistent with your goals, age and risk comfort level. It's a lot like driving a car. When the country is in a recession (a downward movement in economic activity), when things are gloomy and you can't see potential dangers and detours in the road ahead, it's time to cut your speed to about 30 percent in stocks. Then, when the sun shines again and you have a clearer view of what lies ahead, you can increase your speed to 60-70 percent in stocks.

Use Dollar/Cost Averaging

What goes up must come down. Dollar/cost averaging is a simple strategy to smooth out the up and down swings in the market and to keep you from doing what other investors do. Not wanting to be left out in a bull market (when the stock market is experiencing good times and companies have rising share prices), they jump right in after a couple of 'up' days on the Dow Jones Index. On what is called a 'correction',* or a 'downturn,' in the market, they panic. With a cry of "Get me out of here!" they sell at the low point. (What you don't want to do. Selling at a high yields the most profit.)

Instead of getting on and off that roller coaster, dollar cost-average your investments. Select one or two good no-load mutual funds** and invest a fixed amount in each per month, or alternate. Research shows that over time, in rising markets, this strategy outperforms most other investment strategies.

If you want to enhance performance even more, simply increase your investments when the market is down. Notice how far you'll drive to buy a car, a stereo, or anything else on sale, at a bargain or discount. When a perfectly good stock or mutual fund goes down, however, we tend to shy away.

Don't become caught up in market psychology. Take a long-term perspective and know that the stock market has, over time, outperformed all other types of investments.

Invest in the Dow Stocks That Pay the Highest Dividends

Review the dividend yields among the Dow Jones Index, buy the top-ten yielding stocks, and continue to monitor them. Sell stocks as they drop from the highest-yielding group and replace them so you

---

* correction – technical term used by stock brokers and the like to identify a quick unexpected drop in market value; the thought is the prices were over-valued before and now they have been corrected.

** no-load mutual funds – A 'load' is the commission paid to purchase a mutual fund. 'No load' means no commissions are paid to a stockbroker or financial planner for their assistance in your purchase of the fund.

continue to hold the top ten. These companies tend to have the best long-term performances.

Get Ready to Retire

Even if the Social Security system remains fully intact in the next two decades, it will only provide enough for a meager standard of living after you stop working. The ball is in your court. Determine what retirement benefits are available to you where you work and contribute to the maximum. You may or may not get a current tax deduction for your contribution. That's not nearly as important as the fact that that money is appreciating annually, but you aren't paying taxes on that annual appreciation (until you begin to withdraw those funds at retirement). I can't tell you the sense of relief I've heard from clients who know that they are putting something away toward retirement. It might not be much, but at least it's something!

While you may apply any or all of these ideas and suggestions in the coming years, I hope you will continue to use the tools you have been given in this book. Communicate honestly about money, draw on each other's strengths, and accept your differences.

The best strategy is to work together to make the most of your money instead of letting it become a force to drive you apart.

If you and your partner have a story or strategy that has helped you resolve money conflicts or manage money better, I would love to hear from you. Please drop me a note at Keller, Coad & Collins Investment Counsel Inc., 18300 Von Karman, Suite 640, Irvine CA 92612. My very best wishes to YOU!

Glossary

appreciation – I understand this as when a significant other acknowledges you for something you did. In the world of money and finance it represents the increased value of an investment, such as a rise in your home value, or stock you might own.

balance sheet – The form which lists everything an individual or couple own, and everything they owe. Not to be confused with bedding sheets.

Blue Chip Stocks – Refers to the large familiar corporations which have been around a long time, like IBM, General Motors, 3M and so on.

Bonds – Simply an IOU. The certificate can be issued by the government or a corporation and describes the terms of the loan.

Bull market – When the stock market is experiencing good times and companies have rising share prices. Opposite: Bear market

Cash flow statement – a method of presentation which shows money that has come in and shows where it has been spent.

CD – Certificate of Deposit. When you place your money in the bank and promise not to take it out for some specific period of time, like 3 or 6 months, or 1 or more years. It pays higher interest than a standard savings account, and charges penalties if you want your money sooner than you agreed.

Compensation package – The full list of benefits paid to someone which could include salary, bonus, health insurance, retirement plan contributions, options to buy employer stock at a discount, and so on.

Correction – Technical term, (like when a baby says "poo-poo") used by stockbrokers and the like to identify a quick unexpected drop in market value. The thought is the prices were over-valued before and now they have been corrected.

Dividends – This is the profit after the taxes, a corporation shares with the stockholders. It is stated as an amount per share owned, such as $1.16 per share. Can be paid quarterly, semi–annually or annually.

DOW – Term used to refer to the next definition.

Dow Jones or Dow 30 Industrials – The most frequently quoted index which has 30 household company names such as Disney, McDonalds, Coca Cola, etc. Supposedly designed to measure the health of the economy based on the products manufactured and sold by these corporations. Its validity as an accurate gauge is widely debated.

Forbes – A monthly financial magazine.

Gross National Product (GNP) – It is the total dollar value of all of the goods and services produced by the country in a year.

Illiquid – When an investment cannot be easily converted into cash.

Inflation – The concept which pays the price of goods and services will cost more in the future than they do today. Does not apply to all consumer products. Usually expressed as a percentage per year increase.

Limited Partnership – A form of ownership for an investment. Can be in areas such as real estate, oil and gas exploration, or cable TV broadcasting. Has a general partner who has management responsibilities and decision making authority. The limited partner puts up the money and no other responsibility or authority. If the investment goes bad, or there is liability from any action, their loss is *limited* to the amount invested, and nothing more. This structure is illiquid.

Liquid holding – Cash or assets which can easily and quickly be converted to cash. Opposite: Real Estate, limited partnerships, antiques or art objects.

MBA – Masters in Business Administration

Money Market Account – A stock brokerage account similar to a standard savings account at a bank. Generally pays higher interest and can allow check writing privileges.

Mutual Funds – A group of stocks, bonds or other securities managed by a professional investment manager or company. Often, the stock of 50 corporations or more is purchased. The fund offers diversification, liquidity and can pursue various objectives from blue-chip, high technology, to forest products or utilities.

Net worth – The amount of money you would have left over if you add up everything you own and subtract everything you owe.

No load Mutual Funds – A load is the commission paid to purchase a mutual fund. No load means no commissions are paid to a stockbroker or financial planner for their assistance in your purchase of the fund.

on margin – Where the brokerage firm loans the investor money to buy stock, similar to making a downpayment and financing your car; usually limited to 50% of the value of the stock.

OTC stocks – Over the counter stocks. Generally the lower valued stocks are traded on this exchange versus those traded on the American or New York Stock Exchange.

Portfolio – The term used to describe someone's investment holdings as a group. Can include stocks, bonds, mutual funds, real estate and other businesses owned.

Rate of Return – The percentage amount of earnings received on an investment whether from interest or dividends.

recession – When there is a downward movement in a country's economic activity. This would be acknowledged if the Gross National Product (GNP) has two successive quarterly drops.

S&L – Savings & Loan Institution.

sell at a low point – what you *don't* want to do—the opposite of selling when prices go higher; selling at a high yields the most profit.

Stop-loss order – you would request this of your stock broker to protect you if you guessed wrong on the direction that the market would go. As an example, you could say, "If the stock goes as low as 50 (or any price you chose) sell my shares to save me from more losses."

Total Return – The percentage amount of increase in the value of an investment. This includes interest, dividends and increase in the investments' value (such as stock price rise or real estate appreciation).

Treasuries, long term – These are government issued debt obligations of 1 year or longer. You can loan our government money and they will pay you interest. It is done through Treasury Bills, Bonds and Notes.

Utilities – Stock of power-generation companies, telephone or other areas where you would expect to pay your utility bill.

Venture capital – Money used to start a business. Can come from the individual or outside investors.

Wall Street – Term used to identify where the action takes place in the U.S. stock market. Like referring to the advertising business as Madison Ave.

About the Author

D r. VICTORIA F. COLLINS is a Certified Financial Planner (CFP) and holds a Ph.D. in psychology. She is a recognized leader in the field of financial planning for life transitions. She is active in both the International Association for Financial Planning and the Institute of Certified Financial Planners. A frequent guest on national TV and radio programs, Victoria has appeared on "Good Morning America," the Phil Donahue Show, CBS Network News, and CNN, and in publications such as *The Wall Street Journal, Business Week, Vogue, Glamour, USA Today* and *Money Magazine.* Dr. Collins co-hosted the thirteenth-part PBS special, "The Financial Advisers," and appears daily on OCN's "MoneyWise." She was named one of the nation's top 200 financial advisors by *Worth Magazine* in 1996 and 1997.

Books by Victoria F. Collins

Couples and Money
A Couples' Guide for the New Millennium

Divorce and Money

Smart Ways to Save Money Before and After Divorce

Your Next Fifty Years,
A New Way to Look at How, When and Whether to Retire

SUZANNE BLAIR BROWN is a journalist and former editor of San Diego magazine.

Index

Additional Products to Support Your Financial and Emotional Growth

1. *Wealth On Any Income*, by Rennie Gabriel, CLU, CFP. This book is designed to assist people in creating work as a choice, instead of a requirement. It covers the emotional and practical keys to handling money effectively.

Learn how to:

- ❑ Be rich on any income.
- ❑ Live within your income in 90 days, guaranteed!
- ❑ Get out of credit card debt, easily and forever.
- ❑ Handle emergency spending without creating a financial disaster.
- ❑ Save 10 - 20% of income, and have it in the bank or investments.
- ❑ Set and achieve financial, career, or any goals, and have others support you.

Publication date May, 1998 Retail $14.95 plus sales tax. To order call (800) 940-2622

2. *Wealth On Any Income*. This two hour cassette tape and workbook program guides people through the process of establishing their financial goals, setting up a spending plan (instead of budget), structuring credit card debt to eliminate it, creating a technique to know how much money you have for any category of expenses in less than 10 seconds, without a computer, and much, much more. Program investment of $59 includes the workbook. Call (800) 940-2622

3. *Couples and Money, A Couples' Guide for the New Millennium*, by Victoria F. Collins. $13.95. To order additional copies of this book, call (800) 940-2622.

4. *Divorce and Money*, by Victoria F. Collins. $26.95 Published by Nolo Press (800) 992-6656.

5. *Your Next Fifty Years, A New Way to Look at How, When and Whether to Retire*, by Victoria F. Collins. Published by Henry Holt and available in most book stores. $14.95

6. *Success Club information package*. The success club is designed from the work of Tony Robbins, Wayne Dyer, Brian Tracy, Zig Ziglar, Barbara Sher, Andrew Carnegie, Napoleon Hill and other leaders in the field of human development and achievement. Monthly meetings allow a group of success minded people to support and empower one another through a pre-established structure to achieve goals, not just set them. To request a cassette tape and information package ($5.00) call (800) 940-2622.